Making Friends with Yourself & Other Strangers

Books by Dianna Daniels Booher

Coping . . . When Your Family Falls Apart
Rape: What Would You Do If . . . ?

Making Friends with Yourself & Other Strangers

Dianna Daniels Booher

Julian Messner
New York

Manufactured in the United States of America

Design by Irving Perkins Associates

Library of Congress Cataloging in Publication Data

Booher, Dianna Daniels.
  Making friends with yourself and other strangers.

  Bibliography: p.
  Includes index.
  Summary: Explains how to make new friends, how
to get along in social, group, and dating situations,
how to like and improve oneself, and how to cope
with depression and rejection.
  1. Friendship—Juvenile literature. 2. Self-respect—Juvenile literature. 3. Self-acceptance—
Juvenile literature. 4. Adolescent psychology—
Juvenile literature. [1. Friendship. 2. Inter-
personal relations. 3. Self-acceptance. 4. Psychol-
ogy] I. Title.
BF724.3.F64B66 1982   158'.2   82-60650
ISBN 0-671-45878-7

FOR MY SON, JEFF

Contents

Part One

How to Make Friends Out of Strangers

Chapter One

WHAT'S SO SPECIAL ABOUT FRIENDSHIP?

IF FRIENDS ARE so much work, then why bother? Is it really necessary to good mental health to have friends? That's a question I asked 215 high school students who participated in a survey on friendship. All but three of the students said that friendship was essential, and the majority went on to say that friendship was the most important relationship in their lives. Maybe that's because friendship is a relationship we freely choose to satisfy our specific personal needs. Our parents, brothers, and sisters were "given" to us. In fact, researchers S. Kon Igor and Vladimir Losenkov found that teens, when asked who understood them best, ranked their close friends higher than mother, father, or favorite teacher.

What does friendship do for you?

Most important, friends make you feel better about yourself:

• When I moved my freshman year and didn't have any friends, I got very depressed and didn't care about school. I gained weight and I didn't feel good about myself at all.— *Denonda, 16*

• One of the best presents God could have ever given us.—*Kathi, 17*

• Someone you can't wait to tell your latest news to.—*Vincent, 18*

• Caring about people who care about you.—*Phyllis, 17*

• Being willing to be there—whenever needed or unneeded.—*Christy, 17*

• A link between two people who care, honor, trust, and respect one another.— *Frank, 17*

• Enlightening.—*Brenda, 16*

• Knowing a person well enough to predict what they will say or think without becoming identical. It is growing your own ways and growing together.—*Marcia, 16*

• Someone to turn to when you are in need or just someone to party with.— *Scott, 17*

• Someone you can count on, laugh with, cry with, or just be with and not say a word, and still be happy.—*Nina, 17*

Relationships such as these don't just happen; they take hard work. That astonishes some people, but it really shouldn't. Consider that few other areas of life just happen to turn out well without effort. In school, don't you study for tests, hand in your homework, and take notes in class to get good grades? In sports, don't you memorize plays and exercise your muscles to stay in shape? One teen makes this analogy: "Friendship is like a slow-growing plant. It takes lots of time and energy."

   • Without friends you have no self-confidence and may commit suicide or a crime—anything to get some attention.— *Daaron, 15*
   • If I had no friends, I would wonder why? Am I not nice or is something wrong with me?—*Heather, 16*
   • I need to feel liked by others to appreciate myself.—*Becky, 18*
   • I have a brother who got kicked out of his group. Now he is very obnoxious at home.—*Allison, 17*

Second, friends support you in becoming your best self:

   • You need someone to cheer you up, listen to you, help in problems—things a mother used to do. But a peer makes things sink in better.—*Teresa, 16*
   • Friends are teachers, helpers, molders, all in one.—*John, 15*
   • Friends are important to your security and your school grades.—*Matt, 16*
   • My friends keep me away from drugs, beer, and things like that.—*Greg, 16*
   • Friends teach you to communicate better, to defend yourself, and to respect others.—*Jason, 18*

Some people have the idea that the need for friendship fades as you get older. Barry, 18, says: "I think you get used to not having friends, and you grow out of chumming around. Friends become just acquaintances." But from my own experience and from that of countless others, friendship is a lifelong need, very necessary to good mental health. Other teens agree:

> • About two summers ago some guys I was hanging around with decided to give me the cold shoulder and that was the worst summer of my life. I had nothing to do except smoke cigars and watch TV.—*Blake, 18*
> • Anyone who has no friends would go insane.—*Scharron, 16*
> • Friends are as important as food and water. If you didn't have them, you couldn't survive.—*Carrie, 17*

WHEN AND WHERE TO FIND FRIENDS

In a word, you can find friends everywhere. The key is to be available. Some kids complain about having no friends, but then do everything possible to keep from meeting people. They arrive at school just in time to walk into first period; they eat at the same place every day; they don't join any clubs, teams, or committees; they go straight home after school and stay there until their schedule forces them to return to school the next morning.

New students particularly must fight the hideaway syndrome. Vance Packard, while researching for his *Nation of Strangers*, found that the average person moves fourteen times in his/her lifetime. When you think of friends, you can't think in past tense. Friends need to be present. But newcomers can take the initiative by joining programmed activities like scouts, church youth groups, school clubs, and city or school sports leagues. When you meet people in these groups, you know that you have at least one common interest that can lead to conversation, which, in turn, can eventually lead to friendship.

However, even after making an initial attempt to join these types of activities, some teens still complain that they don't make friends. This usually happens when they put physical or emotional distance between themselves and those around them.

For instance, in the cafeteria a person might sit at the end of the table, leaving only one side or none open for someone else to sit down. Sometimes, he makes sure there are empty seats between him and others. Or he may even pile books or coats on those chairs so no one else can sit down by him. Other teens look the other way when someone approaches, as if they are deep in concentration or interested in the scenery outside, or they bury their heads in a book. These are physical ways people, consciously or uncon sciously, make themselves unavailable for meeting others.

In addition to being physically unavailable,

many teens make themselves *emotionally* unavailable because they don't want to get involved. Philip Zimbardo, in his book *Shyness*, calls this living by the gold plated rule: "Give nothing to others as you would have them give nothing to you." Teens who live by this rule make no commitments of their time, energy, or ego, and in return they have no responsibilities or favors to give.

Still others try to insulate themselves emotionally from the pain of rejection. But to find a friend, you have to risk rejection. You have to smile and accept the possibility that no one may smile back. You may ask for directions to the water fountain and get your answer wrapped in a bothered tone. You may compliment a hairdo and get a snub. You may comment on the soccer game and get a blank stare. But the pain of this kind of rejection really is short-lived—maybe five to fifteen minutes. The embarrassment will pass and you can get on with your life. What's fifteen minutes compared with a lifetime of friendlessness? Fear of that uncomfortable feeling should not hold you back from attempting friendship.

Schedule people into your life, physically and emotionally.

CASUAL, CLOSE, INTIMATE— WHICH ONE ARE YOU?

When I asked the survey group of high schoolers if friends ever misused them, they quickly related some of the pain caused by "friends":

- They don't admit we're friends when we're out with someone else they want to impress.
- This girl and I spent a lot of time together and we became good friends. Then she got a boyfriend and I don't hear from her anymore.
- I have a friend who always makes fun of me in front of others to make himself look better.
- They come around only when they need me, when they feel insecure. When I need them, they're not available.
- I don't like being dumped on. They pour out their problems on me and expect me to help. I don't care that much.
- Sometimes they try to put things over on you and use you to get to someone else. One of my ex-boyfriends used me to get to the top of the "social ladder." When I realized it, she didn't make it.
- This one girl used me to get concert tickets. Even a date with my brother.
- One girl used to hang around me just to get revenge on her ex-boyfriend.
- I have one friend who calls when she and her other friend want to go skating and they have no transportation. They invite me along and guess who drives?

These comments and many more like them from respondents on the survey indicate that many teens do not understand the different levels of friendship. Thus, they are frequently disappointed and hurt because they've expected some-

thing of a "friend" that didn't materialize—
loyalty, companionship, a listening ear, gratitude.
As a teen you've already passed through several
"stages" in your understanding of friendship.
When you were in preschool, you saw friendships
as "encounters." You played with another child
one day, went home and that was that until you
happened to meet again. And when you and your
friend were together, everything revolved around
your needs—what toy you wanted and where you
wanted to play. But when you got into the older
elementary grades, the second stage of friendship, you began to see your friend's point of view
and to share secrets, plans, feelings, and solutions
to problems. Finally, only as you reached your
teen years, the third stage, have you begun to see
the complex relationship friendship really is. As a
teen you see needs that friends can meet. And you
also understand your need for independence.

Part of the understanding about that complex-
ity, though, is being aware of the different levels
of friendships you'll have all your life. To avoid
disappointment, you have to lay your expectations on the table.

ACQUAINTANCES.

Acquaintances are classmates you recognize in
the hall, kids who ride the same bus as you do
every day, neighbors who live on your street,
people who take piano from the same teacher you
have, friends of friends.

To categorize these relationships, ask yourself

these questions: Do you go out of your way to strike up a conversation with this person? Do you know his/her telephone number?

CASUAL FRIENDS.
These are friends who come into your life because of a special interest or a common purpose. You both get put on the decorations committee for the prom; you are on the swim team together; you both discuss how you hate chemistry and compare notes before and after class. If you remove this one interest or activity from your life, you'd probably have little to say and would probably stop seeing each other.

To categorize these relationships, ask yourself these questions: What would you talk about if this one activity dropped out of your life? Would you tell this person how much you cried when your pet died?

CLOSE FRIENDS.
These are friends you chum around with. You go to the movies with them, you shop with them, you have pizza at your house and theirs. You may have no special interests other than talking and sharing your feelings, thoughts, ambitions. You can argue and express differing opinions without being afraid you'll destroy the friendship.

To categorize these relationships, ask yourself these questions: Can you be together without talking and still be comfortable? Would you feel offended if this friend didn't call to congratulate you on being elected All-State?

INTIMATE FRIENDS.

If an intimate friend didn't call to congratulate you, you would be worried rather than hurt that he hadn't called. This person has the freedom to tell you "the truth" no matter how it hurts, because you know he only has your best interest at heart. He or she is interested in improving your character and seeing you reach your goals. This friend would give up a ski weekend to be with you if your mother died.

To categorize this friend, ask yourself these questions: Would this person agree with you that "just this once" going off your diet wouldn't hurt, or would he get you out of the house and away from food? Could you tell this friend how badly you are hurting over your parents' divorce? Could you tell this friend that he's being childish and petty in his relationship with his dad?

Hurt feelings and disappointments creep in when you confuse the type of friendship you have with someone. As Adelaide Bry says, in her book *Friendship*, "Fair-weather friends are fun for fair weather." Don't expect sacrifice from a casual friend and you won't be disappointed. If the stakes are high, don't expect a casual friend to keep your secrets. When an acquaintance passes you in the shopping mall and doesn't remember your name, don't feel insulted. When a casual friend forgets to call when you're sick, remember that your welfare is not his life's work. When an intimate friend tells you that you've become a snob, listen rather than pout. As your relationship grows from level to level, you can expect more, receive more, and give more support and love.

ARE ALL FRIENDS CREATED EQUAL?

For the most part, yes. We tend to pick friends we consider our equals. Age, race, sex, and social status influence our choice of friends. Friends help us feel good about ourselves because they reflect our own values and interests. If you make good grades in school, you don't knowingly choose a friend who thinks intelligent people are no fun.

This is not to say that you and all your friends have exactly the same personality traits and interests—only that you don't contradict each other's goals, values, and self-concept.

Inequalities sometimes put unnecessary strain on the relationship. For instance, if one person has less money to spend and lives in a less expensive house, he may feel self-conscious about having his friend stay overnight or feel embarrassed that he can't buy as nice a birthday present as he received from the friend. On the other hand, the richer person may want to go someplace where tickets cost more than his friend can afford, and he has to choose between missing the event or going without the friend.

If you become friends with a disabled person "as a favor," both of you will end up resenting the relationship. Only if your friendship is equal in other ways will you be able to develop a satisfying relationship.

When making friends with someone of the opposite sex, you always run into the problem of an unequal relationship if one of you wants to be more than "just friends." That is why, generally, girls can be closer to their girlfriend's boyfriend than they can be to an unattached boy. There's less chance of one having more intense feelings for the other than "just friendship."

All this is not to say that "unequal" friendships can't work out. For instance, a teen may be friends with an older adult. The adult may give mature advice, extra support, intellectual stimulation, while the teen gives a sense of pride and fun. A richer friend may give financial help (buy the movie ticket or dinner or lend money) while the poorer friend may supply emotional strength (helping the friend communicate better with classmates or showing love the friend doesn't get from parents).

Such relationships can work fine. The key is that they be *mutually satisfying*.

FRIENDSHIPS WITH THE OPPOSITE SEX

Are friendships with the opposite sex different from friendships with the same sex? Eighty percent of the girls and eighty-eight percent of the boys surveyed said "yes." How are they different? Here's what the boys had to say:

On activities and interests:

- With boys you can go out and raise hell. You can't with a girl in the car.
- With males I'm a lot rowdier, louder, than with female friends. With other males we usually surf, play football, and things like that. With females I usually just sit around and talk.

On conversations:

- With male friends I usually just talk about things we're going to do. Girls can talk about feelings, too.
- It takes more tact to talk to the opposite sex.
- I tend to be more complimentary, more friendly, and more attentive while talking to girls.
- Some things guys talk about you just couldn't tell females.

On the relationship in general:

- With the opposite sex, you flirt; with the same sex, you just kid around.
- I'm much more gentle and loving, not bossy or leading, with girls.
- Friendships with the opposite sex are more intimate and caring.
- I act in a much more mature fashion and change personalities. With guys, who cares?
- I'm real nice with women. I just kind of take it easy with guys.

Here's what the girls had to say about their friendships with boys:

On activities and interests:

- You have different interests. Girls go shopping a lot and one guy and one girl would not likely do that.
- I'm not as wild when I'm around boys.

On conversations:

- Guys are easier to talk to about other guys. A guy can answer more questions and tell you if you're choosing the right person.
- With my friends who are girls, I talk more about personal things in my life. With my friends who are boys, I talk more about things *they* would be interested in.
- In conversations with the opposite sex, there's always the "cutesy side."
- It's easier to talk more freely and openly and give your true feelings with boys than

girls, because girls judge what you say and you can't be as open.
- I don't tell males my darkest and deepest secrets. With them, things are more casual.

On the relationship in general:

- Friendships with girls are more serious; with guys you are shallow.
- Girls are more like sisters; they're part of you.
- With girls you're not as self-conscious.
- Boys seem to gossip less.
- My friendships with boys are better because I can hug them and kiss them freely when I'm happy. Nowadays if I hugged or kissed a girl, society would be shocked.
- Friendships with girls are more sincere. With boys, you usually kind of flirt and tease.
- I can be myself around guys, not so with girls. The girlfriends I have are more apt to judge me. They criticize me behind my back. I have only one girlfriend I can really be myself with.
- Guys are less complicated than girls. With girls, it's like an instinct that you have to compete with them and always be on your guard.
- Guys are more caring about your feelings. They make you feel more worth something. You don't have peer pressure from them either. I value more my friends who are of the opposite sex.

You can see that friendships with the opposite

sex often bring out either the best or the worst in both sexes. Boys say that friendships with girls allow them to get in touch with inner feelings and emotions without the pressure to be "macho" with other males. They tend to be nicer, more mature, more loving, more gentle and more protective with girls. Girls say that with boys they can be more open without worrying about gossip, judgments, betrayals, or competition from other girls. Friendships with boys also allow more physical expression of affection essential to development.

Yet, for many, friendships with the same sex allow more freedom to be themselves and to share intimate feelings without self-consciousness and complicated flirting.

Conclusions? Friends of both sexes can add much to your emotional and mental growth toward complete, healthy, mature adult relationships.

QUALITY VERSUS QUANTITY

Some kids are so anxious to be accepted and popular that they flit from one group to another trying to be friends with everybody. As a result, they have a number of acquaintances and casual friends, but few meaningful relationships with close and intimate friends. Of the 215 students in the survey, on the average they reported having 2.5 intimate friends.

Several (11) said they had no intimate friend at all. Evelyn, 16, says, "Everyone needs an emotional outlet and friends are helpful in that respect. I do not require them and I go through periods of time when I do not need a friend. I never like to be dependent on people for anything."

On the other extreme, Pat, 15, says, "I don't think it's necessary for everyone to have friends, but then some people like me *must* have lots of friends."

If acquaintances and casual friends meet your needs, then you need simply to get involved in school, church, club activities and find a common interest. On the other hand, if you go in for quality and want more close and intimate friends, you'll need to work at those friendships by devoting more thought, time, and energy to the relationships.

HOW GOOD A FRIEND ARE YOU?

"The only way to have a friend is to be one," Emerson wrote. Below are several situations in which you may find yourself from time to time. Check the response closest to the one you would make in the given circumstances; then read the text below the situations to determine what kind of friend you are.

SITUATION #1:

You've planned to go to a movie with a friend, but someone you enjoy being with more calls at the last minute and asks you to go out. You would:

A. Go out with the second friend and make up an excuse why you can't make the movie with your first friend.
B. Go out with the second friend and tell the truth about why you've changed plans.
C. Tell the second friend you can't go because you've already made plans.

SITUATION #2:

A friend wants to date a boy her parents won't let her go out with and whose friendship you think is harmful for her. She asks if she can tell her parents that she is with you on Friday night instead of with the boyfriend. You would:

A. Say okay, because she will get angry if you criticize her choice of dates and refuse her the favor.
B. Reason with her about doing something behind her parents' back and try to persuade her that the boy is not right for her. If she is not persuaded, you would go through with what she asked of you.
C. If she did not agree with your reasoning, you would refuse to let her lie about you anyway. At least, you would be doing all you could to keep her out of the harmful relationship.

SITUATION #3:

Your friend always borrows clothes from you and this time has borrowed a sweater and has not returned it. You would:

    A. Hint about the sweater and hope he/she returns it.
    B. Discuss the fact that constant borrowing bothers you.
    C. Say nothing because he/she would feel that you were being critical.

SITUATION #4:
One of your friends has a new haircut which you think looks unattractive. You would:

    A. Compliment him/her on the change to make him/her feel good.
    B. Say exactly what you think—that it looks bad.
    C. Be tactful, mentioning the good things (that the style should be easy to keep) and the bad things (that it may be a little too short this time, but it can be cut a little longer next time).

SITUATION #5:
You're with a group of kids who begin to criticize an absent friend of yours. You would:

    A. Keep quiet and try to change the subject.
    B. Defend the absent friend.
    C. Smile, nod, and try to make a joke of the things they say.

SITUATION #6:

You're attracted to someone your best friend is dating. You would:

A. Tell the friend and hope he/she understands that you can't help the attraction and what may happen.
B. Don't tell the friend and try to stay away from the other person until you know they are no longer interested in each other.
C. Let the opposite-sex person know you are attracted and hope they will break up soon.

SITUATION #7:

A friend makes a tactless remark that hurts your feelings. You would:

A. Get angry and break up the friendship.
B. Give the silent treatment until he/she figures out what is wrong and apologizes.
C. Admit that your feelings are hurt and discuss the issue.

SITUATION #8:

A friend of yours whose parents divorced a year ago continues to call almost every night to unload all his bitter feelings on you. You would:

A. Listen as long as the friend needs you because the crisis can't go on forever, can it?
B. Say that you want to help, but that you are

getting too depressed listening to the problem. Ask him/her not to call so often and suggest he/she see a counselor.

C. Break off your friendship because you can't devote that much time to the phone calls and don't want to be depressed all the time. You never explain why you are pulling away because you would feel too guilty and you don't want to hurt the person.

SITUATION #9:

Both you and your friend have planned to take a Saturday course with a tennis pro. You call the instructor first and he says he has a place for only one more student. Your friend has been playing tennis for two years and is really serious about the game. You just want to try a new sport and see how you like it. You would:

A. Take the opening since you called first and pretend that you didn't know your friend would be left out.
B. Sign up your friend for the opening because the course means more to him than it does to you.
C. Tell your friend about the problem and see what he says. Maybe he will insist that you take the slot since you called first, or maybe he will refuse to sign up too and you can both wait until something else comes along.

SITUATION #10:

Your friend went to work for a hamburger chain six months before you did, and he got you the job working with him. After another six months, because you have been a dependable employee (unlike your friend who frequently comes late to work) you are offered the job of assistant manager of the night shift. You need the extra money. You would:

A. Turn down the job because your friend might be hurt.
B. Take the job and not say anything to your friend until he finds out for himself.
C. Take the job and diplomatically mention it to your friend yourself, hoping you can discuss how he feels about it and his constant tardiness.

SITUATION #11:

Two of your friends don't like each other. You would:

A. Not plan things when you would be around both of them at the same time, and keep quiet about times you were with the other friend.
B. Choose between the friends and end the relationship with one of them.
C. Plan to get them together as much as possible and try to get them to see each other's good points.

SITUATION #12:

You have a casual friend who could be very useful to you in winning a student council election. You would:

    A. Try to spend more time with this person so that he/she could introduce you to more people.
    B. Continue with the casual relationship as it is because you don't really have much in common with this person.
    C. Drop this person's name around often so that more people will think you are close friends.

SITUATION #13:

You and a friend have been planning a day at the beach for about six weeks, but you constantly wind up with conflicting schedules for Saturday—babysitting jobs, family responsibilities, studying. Finally, both of you clear your calendars for a particular weekend and drive an hour to the beach—only to find heavy rain. You would:

    A. Gripe and complain and stay in a bad mood all day.
    B. Try to see the humor in the situation and make some alternate suggestions about what to do for the day.
    C. Blame your friend for not having been free to go the last weekend when you suggested making the trip.

As you read the following explanations, evaluate your responses to the above situations. Although they are not an exact measure of how good a friend you are, they will help you consider what qualities others expect from you. Also, your responses may reveal what level of friendship exists between you and certain people. Finally, your response will reveal something of your self-control and how it affects your relationships to others.

SITUATION #1:

Response A suggests you are willing to lie and hurt people for selfish reasons. If you chose B, you are honest but perhaps uncaring about hurting other people unnecessarily. Response C says you are an honest, loyal friend who cares about others' feelings.

SITUATION #2:

If you chose Response A, you lack the confidence to stand up for what you feel is right. Eventually, you may grow to resent being used in this way. If you chose B, you are a better friend in that you are willing to risk your friend's anger in order to convince her to make the right (in your opinion) decision. Response C indicates you are probably an intimate friend. You care about your friend's welfare and you respect your own feelings, too. Because you refuse to be an accomplice in the lie, you will not resent the relationship later.

SITUATION #3:

Response A says that you have some concern for your needs but are not assertive enough to express yourself. Your friendship is not stable enough to risk criticism. If you chose B, you are close friends and refuse to let resentment build up between you. Response C suggests you have little respect for your own needs and will probably let resentment grow until the relationship breaks over this or something else later on.

SITUATION #4:

Response A is dishonest. Although you care about making the person feel good about himself/herself, you are not a close enough friend to be of real help. Response B says that you take your friendship for granted and maybe are callous about hurting others' feelings. Response C says that you have your friend's best interest at heart and that you hope your friend will become more attractive by modifying the hairstyle, but you do not want to be brutal in your comments to the point of causing unnecessary pain about something that can't be changed now.

SITUATION #5:

Response A says although you feel loyal to the friend, you do not have the ego strength to risk possible rejection on your friend's behalf. Response B suggests that you are a loyal friend. Response C indicates that you are highly insecure and only a casual friend.

SITUATION #6:

Response A indicates that you are an honest person, but that you have your own interest at heart and are unwilling to sacrifice for the sake of friendship. Response B says that you are not close friends; therefore, you can't share the problem, but at least you are trying to be considerate and respectful. Response C indicates someone who is only a casual friend and feels no loyalty.

SITUATION #7:

Response A means that you do not value the friendship because you are ready to jump to the worst conclusion possible—that your friend intentionally hurt you. Response B indicates that you do not mind jeopardizing the friendship by letting resentment build. Response C indicates that you are close or intimate friends and you want to clear up the misunderstanding so your relationship can continue to grow.

SITUATION #8:

Response A suggests that you are a caring friend, but you are too passive in looking after your own needs—especially if your time is monopolized and you become depressed. Response B suggests that you are close or intimate friends and' your friendship is approaching the danger zone. You feel free to suggest a solution for your friend's own best interest. Response C indicates that you are assertive about your own rights, but that you are not close friends because you offer no solution and no explanation to your friend.

SITUATION #9:
Only a casual friend or acquaintance would make Response A; self-interests definitely come into play here. Response B indicates that you are intimate friends because you are willing to sacrifice something unimportant to you to further your friend's goal. You do not even discuss the dilemma first because you know your friend would probably insist that you take the opening and you do not want to put him in that position. Response C says that you are probably close friends and hate putting your own interest before your friend's. However, you probably hope he will insist you take the opening, or put off the class so you won't feel guilty about the situation.

SITUATION #10:
Response A says that you are putting your friend's interest ahead of yours to the point of hurting yourself. If you really need the money, resentment may soon build between you. Response B says you are only casual friends, and you do not

care enough to spare the friend's feelings by telling him/her first. Response C suggests that you are a close friend and care about each other's feelings. However, you know that you must not sacrifice a job you need because of your friend's irresponsibility. You realize that turning down the job would not ensure that your friend would get it instead. Perhaps you can even help your friend change his habits for the future.

SITUATION #11:

Response A says you are not strong enough to risk rejection by either friend but that you care about both friends' feelings. Response B says you are letting one friend manipulate you. Response C says that you are enough of your own person to risk disapproval to continue both friendships. You are close friends with both and care deeply about each relationship.

SITUATION #12:

Response A indicates dishonesty and the willingness to "use" the friend. Response B shows that you are a forthright person and will not compromise your own integrity. You respect others. Response C suggests that you are still not completely honest about the friendship, and you do not have much confidence to win the election on your own.

SITUATION #13:

Response A says that your disposition may be as cloudy as the day; you will probably contribute to your friend's gloom. Response B suggests that you have a good sense of humor, even when disappointed, and that your friends probably like being around you no matter what. Response C indicates that you have not learned to handle disappointment on your own and that you don't mind risking a friendship when you're in a rotten mood.

On the survey, more than half of the teens listed honesty and trust as the most desirable qualities in a friend. Following close behind were loyalty, understanding, caring, consideration, and a sense of humor. How do you rate as a friend?

RULES FOR BUILDING A MEANINGFUL FRIENDSHIP

1. SPEND TIME TALKING.

Consider the amount of time you spend in honest conversation with your friends. How much of your "together" time is spent watching TV or a movie, playing a sport, doing homework? Sure, you *can* talk about important, personal things while something else is going on, but do you? Rather than getting to know each other's feelings, thoughts, ideas, goals, are you just together physically? To develop a closer relationship, try spending more time doing things that require little concentration so that you can lavish attention on each other—like eating together, walking, jogging, or riding somewhere together. Enjoy a hobby together, go to the beach, shop.

2. BE INTERESTED.

Dale Carnegie advises: "You can make more friends in two months by becoming interested in other people than you can in two years by trying to get other people interested in you." The same advice goes for making close friends out of casual ones. If you don't know enough about someone to be interested in what's going on in his life, ask questions. How does he spend his time? Where did he used to live? To what neat places has he been? What does he plan to do next year? After high school? After college? Nothing makes a potential friend glow brighter than having someone really interested in what matters to him.

3. BE OPEN.

To have friends be honest and open with you—in effect, to give part of themselves to you—you must be willing to do the same. If you aren't willing to share personal thoughts, dreams, or opinions with others, don't expect your friendship to ever go beyond the casual mark. Jess Lair, in his book, *I ain't much, baby—but I'm all I've got*, writes: "I didn't want close personal friends because they'd be too close to me and I couldn't stand the self-awareness a close relationship would force on me. And I realized I wouldn't want to be a friend of mine. A friend of mine was somebody I took off the shelf, played with for five minutes, and then put back on the shelf. . . ."

In being real, you have to chance rejection and misunderstanding. Keeping secrets about yourself and your life draws a barrier beyond which your friends feel like trespassers.

As a high school junior, I worked at an amusement park where I became friends with Linda. Before the summer was out, we shared problems and concerns about school, boys, and family. But the first Friday night we double-dated and she asked me to stay overnight afterward, our relationship hit a snag. Imagine my shock when her severely disabled little brother rolled into the room in his wheelchair. She had never mentioned having a brother!

After spending the night and the next day at her house, I could tell that she and her brother were very close. Yet, I couldn't get over the fact that she had never even mentioned him to me. Was she embarrassed about his appearance? Was she resentful of the extra attention he needed? Did she think I would like her less if she had a disabled, retarded family member?

The point was that something very important in her life—be it embarrassment, pain, joy, resentment, or love—she had not even discussed with me. Immediately, when I discovered her omission of truth, I knew there were "off-limit" topics to our relationship. Because of her inability to discuss her feelings with me, our relationship took a step backward. We remained only casual friends.

But being open and real doesn't mean spitting out of your mouth everything that runs through your head. Being open or honest doesn't mean telling people off or "letting it all hang out," sparing no feelings. Rather, it means being transparent about yourself.

When friends want advice, they'll usually ask for it. In most cases, they only want support. When I asked teens whether you should always tell the truth to friends, their yes's and no's were about even. Here's what a few had to say:

- I think if you really care about someone, you'll tell them the truth even if it hurts a little.
- I think you should tell the truth, but you don't have to tell the whole truth if it's going to hurt.
- You should always tell the truth and then they'll never doubt you and always will tell the truth back to you.
- Friends are bound to find out the truth, and it's better when they hear it from you.
- To always tell the truth can be harmful. What's important is not to lie.
- If it's beneficial to them, yes. If it's harmful to their self-esteem, no.

In summary, be open and honest about your-self, and let your friend clue you about whether he wants honesty or support at any particular moment. Only an *intimate* friend can take the liberty to tell you the truth when you may not want to hear it.

4. SHOW YOUR APPRECIATION.

Friends, no matter how close, don't want to be taken advantage of. Here are some comments from teens who feel their close friends sometimes misuse them:

- They forget to call when they say they will.
- Like this morning, for instance. My friend said she needed to drop something off at the bank before school, and she'd only be a second. I was driving and said I'd take her but it ended up taking much longer and we were late for school.
- I have some friends who come to me when they're down, but when I need a friend they're not willing to be there for me.
- They talk you into doing their homework for them and then they never even say thanks.
- They always ask me to take them places, but they never offer to buy any gas.

Did you see yourself in any of the comments above? No one—not enemy or lover—likes to be taken for granted. "Friendship is always a sweet responsibility," says Kahlil Gibran, "never an opportunity."

Give sincere compliments; show your appreciation with gifts; return favors.

5. LET YOUR FRIENDS DO THINGS FOR YOU.

This is the other side of the coin. Some people feel uncomfortable having to ask for favors or for time, support, money, or understanding. There is a saying, "The easiest way to lose a friend is to save his life or lend him money." In other words, when someone feels indebted to you, he may feel unworthy to be your friend or embarrassed that he can't repay you. Remember what I said earlier about friendships being mutually satisfying most often when they are equal. No friendship can survive when all the giving is one-sided.

The same goes for favors. People like to feel needed as long as you don't overdo it. Consider the pleasure you feel when you know you've helped tutor someone through algebra. They need that same satisfaction from time to time.

6. DON'T HANG ON TO THE FRIENDSHIP FOR DEAR LIFE.

For friendship to grow, you have to be able to get along without it. To fertilize the growing relationship, you must keep contributing new energy, new spirit, new ideas. To do that, you have to continue to grow as an individual. By the same token, you have to let your friend have the room to grow by developing other friendships and interests apart from you.

If both of you are wrapped up only in each other, you soon become "root-bound" and stifle each other's growth.

Friends make you feel good about yourself, provide help in times of crisis, and give you pleasure. You can find potential friends anywhere as long as you make yourself both physically and emotionally available and take the risk of possible rejection. To make a friend, become one. Understand the various levels of friendship—casual, close, and intimate—and what you can expect from each. Then you won't offend or be disappointed by expecting too much or too little of a relationship.

If you are willing to devote the time, energy, and sacrifice, close and intimate friends are yours for the making.

Chapter Two

HOW TO TALK TO ANYBODY ABOUT ANYTHING

CONSIDER SOME OF the all-time great relationships—Anthony and Cleopatra, Bob Hope and Bing Crosby, Johnny Carson and Ed McMahon. They all had to have their first conversation. To turn strangers and acquaintances into casual, close, or intimate friends, you, too, will have to learn the art of conversation.

Have you ever sat behind two people engaged in a marathon conversation at a concert, movie, or other program? Granted, you were probably annoyed. But then, too, if you have trouble talking with people, you may have been a little envious. But don't delude yourself by thinking that they are naturally talkative extroverts. Many TV personalities, politicians, cheerleaders, and class presidents say they often feel shy and must force themselves to talk to people. Even if you, too, are shy, there's no reason you cannot learn how to carry on a conversation.

47

Let's break down the mysterious art into various stages just as we would any other skill you were about to learn—such as tennis or piano. In tennis, you practice ground strokes and volleys, then work on serves. Reading time signatures comes first in piano, followed by learning the treble-clef notes, the bass-clef notes, the signatures and scales, and finally songs. Put it all together and you're a tennis player or a pianist.

Conversation is much the same. You learn to start one, toss out a few topics, ask questions, respond to listener cues, use body language, and say good-byes. Before you know it, you're a conversationalist. Let's begin.

OPENERS AND INTRODUCTIONS

Contrary to what you may think, people usually will meet you halfway in beginning a conversation. Choose an appropriate time, however—when the person looks approachable, when he or she is not busy and is smiling at you. You can begin with a simple, "Hi, my name is ____," then pause and let that person introduce himself.

And listen. Many people are so concerned with their next line that they miss the person's name. If you don't understand the name, ask the person to spell it. A person's name is music to him, and he's flattered that you want to get it right. If you don't believe it, next time someone mispronounces a name, listen to the irritated tone of voice when the owner corrects him.

After the introduction, you can follow up with a mild, direct, or flippant (occasionally) question or statement about your surroundings or what's happening at the moment.

Mild:

What do you think of the band?

The parking lot sure looks crowded. Wonder how they got such a crowd.

Would you help me find room 22?

Do you know what the score is? I can't see the board.

Are you taking any math courses this year?

I hate waiting in lines, don't you?

Direct:

I've been watching your serve. It's terrific. Could you watch mine and give me a few pointers?

I like your shirt. Is it lightweight enough for the heat in this building?

Would you like to go across the street with me and get something to eat?

I know a friend of yours, Fred Sanders. He said you two see a lot of each other.

Flippant:

(Not recommended on most occasions.) What do you say we leave this movie and create our own scenes? (May sound too forward rather than cute.)

Anybody who would sign up for McWhorter's course has to be a little dim. (What if the person has a friend in that course?)

How are you eating that junk? (Maybe he or she likes it.)

Remember, however, that when you open with a flippant statement or question, you always risk offending the person or having him or her think the remark was dumb rather than cute.

If you've met the person before but can't remember his name, don't be embarrassed to ask again: "I'm _____ and we met before at Davia's party, but I've forgotten your name." Never walk up to somebody and say, "Remember me?" What if he or she doesn't? You've embarrassed the person and destroyed your own self-confidence.

When you've met the person earlier, at a second meeting you can always comment on something that happened the last time you were together: "Remember last game when the referee kept calling illegal-motion penalties all night?" "The band we had last dance was really good, do you remember?" "What did you think of the assignment she gave for last night? How long did it take you to do it?" "Yesterday in class you said something that really makes sense to me (and repeat what he said and how you feel about the issue). The possibilities are endless.

KEEPING THE CONVERSATION ALIVE

The most important thing to remember in keeping the talk flowing is to listen for your next cue. Often people make opening remarks and then fail to listen to the other person's response.

First, remember the importance of eye contact. Signal the person that you are interested in keeping the conversation going—that it was not just an offhand remark—by maintaining eye contact. How many times have you heard a teacher tell the class, "Pay attention," even though no one was distracting or talking? He or she was probably reacting to the lack of eye contact from students, indicating that they were uninterested in what was being said.

When you make an opening comment or question and then let your eyes drift off to the books in your arm or someone across the room, you give the impression that you're waiting for something more interesting to come along. *Look* at the person as if you've been waiting all day just to get this conversation going.

When the other person takes the ball and throws out a new question or statement, make an effort to catch it and don't respond with one word answers.

"Do you like this band?"

Stopper:

"They're okay."

Accepting the pass:

"They're okay. I like the type of things they play, but the bass isn't too good. What do you think?"

"I heard Mr. Sherrill is really hard."

Stopper:

"Oh, really."

Accepting the pass:
>
> "Oh, really. Where did you hear that?" (Or, "Does he give essay tests or why do you say that?")
>
> "This school gets more crowded every year. Looks like they'd hurry and get that new one opened."

Stopper:
>
> "Yeah."

Accepting the pass:
>
> "Yeah, it does. I think the incoming freshman class is a lot larger than last year's." (Or, "Yeah, have you heard what the holdup is on opening the new one?")
>
> "Our football team was so good last year that we'll never be able to beat that record. With a new quarterback especially."

Stopper:
>
> "Really."

Accepting the pass:
>
> "You may be right, but I hear Vernon is pretty good passing. What was our record last year anyway?"
>
> "Is there a Coke machine around here somewhere?"

Stopper:
>
> "I don't know."

Accepting the pass:
> "I don't know. I haven't seen one. You might try down the east hall—I haven't been down that way."

> "I broke the heel off my shoe on the way in here."

Stopper:
> "Hmmmmmmm."

Accepting the pass:
> "That's going to be uncomfortable. What can I do to help?"

You get the idea. Be an active listener and make the person feel that what he has said is important to you. Show that you care, that you want to help, that you want to continue talking to him.

You show a listening attitude not only with words but also with your body language. Keeping your eyes on the person, leaning forward, nodding, and smiling show intense interest. On the other hand, glancing away, excessive movement such as swinging your foot, drumming your fingers, and shifting your position around suggest that you're impatient to get away or that you're bored.

If you strike up a conversation with someone and she fails to give you good listening cues, it may not necessarily mean that she doesn't want to talk. Perhaps your listener, too, is unskilled in conversational tactics. Just be aware of the way these body signals enhance your own conversational skills and keep trying.

TEMPTING TOPICS

The first rule in being a good conversationalist is to be informed. Read your school newspaper, city newspaper, and magazines. See current movies, watch good TV programs, and listen to favorite radio stations for background information about music, events, and trends. Don't completely tune out advertisements either. When someone mentions exercise or diet, you can tell them about a new aerobics class beginning in your area. When someone wears a new blouse collar style, you can comment on that design or other trends in vogue. When someone quotes last night's basketball scores, you'll know the team's standing for the season. Put your mind to work collecting data from all around you, and then you'll be able to "sort and merge" into your own conversations.

On specific topics you can be either factual or personal, make statements or ask questions. Generally, asking questions works best because you involve the other person immediately:

Sports

"Who won the swim meet this weekend?"
"I saw the swim meet this weekend and that was the first time I've ever been to one. I couldn't believe the way . . ."

Hobbies

"How did you get started in collecting autographs?"

"Can you make money doing this or do you primarily do it for fun?"

"Have you ever won any trophies for your racing?"

"Water skiing is so fine. When I'm gliding along, I always feel like a. . . . But I still remember the first time I fell down; I was out at. . . ."

Movies, Books, Music

"I've heard people say *Rickett* was too slapstick; what do you think?"

"Do you know if Barbara Mandrell writes all her own lyrics?"

"I read that book a long time ago, but I still remember this one scene where. . ."

School

"Our school has open campus for lunch, but there's no place to eat nearby. How about your school?"

"Do you know what they do with library fines?"

"What kind of job do you think the Student Council is doing this year?"

Current Events

"What do you think of the air controllers' strike?"

"Do you think most of the Westside is going to vote for Derby or Harris?. . . Why do you say that?"

"I heard the flooding on the other side of
Highway 6 is pretty bad. They've been
evacuating all night. Have you ever had to be
evacuated for anything like that?"

If the other person catches the ball, you'll have
no trouble at all keeping the conversation moving
along these lines. State your opinion about something, then ask how your listener feels about the
subject. Or, ask what your listener thinks and then
state your opinion. And don't be afraid to express
a personal opinion. That's not being egocentric,
but rather open. Personal opinions from you will
usually elicit the same openness in others.

Granted, some of the topics you come up with
may not be the most interesting issues of the year,
but remember that your listener will probably
appreciate any efforts you offer.

A few words of caution:

1. DON'T PRETEND TO BE AN AUTHORITY WHEN YOU'RE NOT.

Chances are you'll be found out much too quickly.
You don't have to be an expert to have someone
interested in what you're saying. And if someone
else brings up a subject of which you know nothing, that doesn't mean you can't talk about it.
Say something like, "I don't know much about the
situation, but I can see where that would cause a
problem. Give me a little background—how did it
all get started anyway?"

2. Avoid Arguments.

If someone expresses an opinion you don't agree with, at least try to see why he feels the way he does. Say something like, "I've never thought of it that way before; you have a point." Or, "I've never heard that before. I'll have to give it some thought." Be careful that your tone says that you respect his right to a differing opinion. No one wins an argument. If you lose, you lose. If you win, you lose.

3. Don't Panic During Silences.

Comfortable silences help you bridge from one topic to the next. Nothing would be more tiring than a sixty-minute, non-stop talker.

BODY LANGUAGE

The person who doesn't understand body language never fully grasps others' moods and meanings. Nonverbal messages can be sent by body movement, space, and posture, as well as by eye contact, voice tone, facial expressions. As a speaker, you must be aware of sending double messages. For instance, if you make a factual statement of something that happened to you on the way to school and then look away from the other person, he probably thinks you don't intend for him to respond. If someone asks a question and you mumble an answer, he may assume you were annoyed by the question.

Watch body language. Yours and theirs. The importance of body language to your conversation can't be overemphasized. Beauty contestants attend classes to learn to sit, walk, stand, and smile to appear attractive and approachable. Politicians hire speech coaches to help them change hand gestures and postures to create various pleasing images. Julius Fast, author of three books on body language, has observed the following messages sent through nonverbal channels:

POSTURE AND MOVEMENT: An uptight person reveals his nervousness by taking a rigidly erect stand. His body muscles tense; his arms often fold across his chest; his facial expression is grim; his movements are quick and jerky. The relaxed person moves and stands comfortably.

POSITION AND SPACE: We use either intimate, personal, social, or public distance to conduct conversations, says Edward Hall in his book, *The Hidden Dimension*. Kissing your boyfriend or girlfriend, arm-wrestling, or letting a friend cry on your shoulder exemplifies *intimate* distance. *Personal* distance, about 1 to 4 feet apart, is used with people we know well to carry on conversations of a personal nature—things you wouldn't want overheard. *Social* distance, about 4 to 12 feet apart, is used in larger groups—at a party, in the hallway at school, in the football stands. *Public* distance, about 12 feet or further apart, is used for more formal speaking like giving a report in front of class.

Problems arise when people violate proper space or territorial lines. If the person you're talking to pulls back or keeps moving his books or a chair between you, perhaps you are standing too close for his comfort. Particularly if your listener doesn't agree with you, he may cross his arms and legs and lean away from you. On the other hand, your listener's use of space can indicate deep interest. He may keep his arms and body loose while sitting or standing near you, and if facing you, lean forward as if to hear better.

TOUCHING, HANDSHAKES, SMILES: Touching people shows that you want to be open to them. Watch good friends, team players, or family members when they are together. They hug, pat, and swat each other. Many people reach out and touch others unconsciously in conversation, indicating warmth and interest. However, be aware if someone seems to recoil when you touch. He may feel that you are invading his privacy.

Handshakes, too, say much about people. A weak, limp handshake comes across like a forced, unpleasant ritual. A firm handshake suggests that the person is confident and willing to meet you halfway in conversation. A macho handshake usually suggests the person is afraid of you and feels the need to prove his strength or get the upper hand either before or after the handshake.

And don't forget to smile. Smiles are instinctive and, says researcher Fast, the only universal body language signal in the world. Plastic smiles don't count for much unless you're in a beauty contest or on a campaign poster. But a warm, genuine smile that says "I like you" will open many doors of friendship.

NERVOUS GESTURES: Rotating a pencil or pen end to end; fidgeting with books, glasses, hair; clearing your throat; tapping your fingers or feet; rubbing your nose; scratching your head; all suggest nervousness. When a listener begins to do these things, try to take more responsibility for the conversation. Change the subject, or compliment him to put him at ease.

VOICE: A mumble suggests disinterest, preoccupation, irritation, or shyness. A loud tone signals enthusiasm, excitement, confidence, or anger. Make sure that your voice tone accurately conveys what you intend.

TIPS FOR TALKING TO SPECIAL PEOPLE ON SPECIAL OCCASIONS

THE PHYSICALLY DISABLED: Keep in mind that a disability is of little significance in conversation on most occasions. Don't talk in pitying tones. Acknowledge the disability, certainly, in the case of hearing impairment. Or, if a blind person needs directions while you are walking or talking together, give them; but don't be overly concerned with the impairment. Make any adjustments necessary and carry on as you would in conversations with anyone else. If the person brings his disability into the discussion, listen to what he has to say. If he doesn't mention the issue, there's no need for you to show concern either.

THE BEREAVED: Seeing someone on the street or

at school after a death in the family always presents a dilemma for the caring individual. You may be hesitant to mention the death for fear of making the person lose his or her composure in public. On the other hand, you feel it is rather coldhearted not to mention the death at all. Generally, it is best to express sympathy briefly and move on to another topic quickly. "I was sorry to hear about your brother's accident. Are you having trouble catching up in your schoolwork now?"

If the person expresses his grief to you in any way, the best thing you can do is to listen with sympathy and understanding. He or she needs to talk about the deceased and pay tribute as a means of working through grief. If the person seems angry and asks questions like why the death had to happen, understand that this too is part of the grief process. You are not expected to have answers. Show you care by simply listening.

vip's: Very Important People in your world may be a congressman scheduled to address your graduating class, a famous musician speaking on career day, or the president of the school board whom you're supposed to usher around on the night of open house.

Barbara Walters gives this advice: You can safely begin with your natural impulse to pay her a compliment, then follow up with a question about her work. "I really like your latest song. Do you write all your own lyrics?" Or, "I read parts of your speech to the Lions Club in the newspaper. Do you find it hard to keep up with a heavy speaking schedule?"

Don't forget that the person, no matter how famous, is human after all. You can always ask about his family or his travel or his comfort.

THE VERY YOUNG: If you find yourself with a younger brother or sister while waiting for a friend, be as warm and friendly as you would if the person were your own age. The main thing to remember is not to talk down to the child and make him feel immature or a pest. You can always ask the child what he likes to do after school, what games he likes to play, what television shows he watches, what does he think of his school, etc.

OLDER PEOPLE: By older people, I mean anyone from parents to grandparents to great-grandparents. Take the opportunity to get to know the parents of your friends and to let them get to know you. Parental disapproval of friends creates problems for many teens. In most cases the issue could be resolved if parents and their children's friends could really get to know one another.

Sincere compliments are a good place to begin. Admire the macrame hanging your friend's mother made or comment on the good-looking boat in the driveway. You can always ask about other children in the family. "Brenda said Michael is coming home from OU next weekend. How does he like campus life?" If you know of some special interest or activity the parent is involved in: "How's the costuming coming for the drama?" People are generally eager to talk about their jobs: "Sherry said you've had to work overtime a lot lately? Are you taking over a new job?"

Don't try to flatter or impress with big words or superior intelligence. Rather, be yourself and express genuine interest just as you would with someone your own age.

ENDING CONVERSATIONS

Don't be brusque in ending a conversation if you want to continue the relationship. For instance, "See you, I've got to go pick up my brother," immediately after the person has said he thinks the sophomore class president has done a lousy job this year, will probably make the person think he has offended you.

Warn the person ahead of time that you need to leave so that he or she can add any last-minute comment necessary. Second, express in some way that you have enjoyed talking, and finally, give intentions to get together again.

To show that you have enjoyed talking to the person, make an outright statement or, better yet, comment on one particular thing he has said that you enjoyed or that you found helpful. "Thanks, I won't forget what you said about how to make a good impression on Ms. Perrot the first day of class." Or, "The joke about the barber was really good; I'll have to remember to tell my dad."

If you really see potential in the relationship, make definite plans to meet again, exchange telephone numbers, offer the person a ride home, or mention your plans for the weekend and ask the person to join you.

Clearly, the person who knows how to introduce himself and open a dialogue, employs active-listening techniques, stays informed about the world around him, is open to express his own opinions, shows interest in others' ideas, and uses appropriate body language will become a good conversationalist. Almost all emotional involvements and meaningful relationships can be traced back to that first line of conversation.

Chapter Three

FITTING INTO A GROUP

WHAT ARE THE pros and cons of belonging to a group? For one thing, being in a group offers security. When you only have one or two friends and they're not around, you can feel pretty much alone. In fact, some kids won't show up to club meetings or social events when one special friend is unable to attend. Having to limit your activities to what one or two others feel like and can do can be a drawback. For that reason, many kids try to have friends in several groups. When one group is not around, they have other friends to have fun with.

Groups can also make you feel good about yourself because you feel that you have something to contribute. They teach loyalty, responsibility, and compromise for a common purpose. But there are disadvantages in belonging to a group. Cynthia, 17, says, "I prefer to dress, talk, and act like myself, not someone from such and such a group."

Some kids may not mind giving up some of their own ideas and values for the sake of belonging; others do. Additionally, loyalty to a group can mean that you are enemies with those outside the group. The others may hint that you should give up activities and other relationships that they don't care for just to be a part of their group. When that's the case, you may have to make the same decision Jason makes: "If I feel like the people in my group are pressing in on me about something, I leave them and find another group."

Others feel as though they belong to a group for reasons outside themselves. The daughter of a pro ball player has this to say about acceptance into her group: "We moved to Colorado for football season every year because my dad played for the Oilers and was traded to the Broncos and we didn't want to live in Colorado all year. I was accepted only because my dad was quarterback with the Broncos." If you feel that the group has ulterior motives for admitting you (a pool in your backyard, ample spending money, a popular older brother), acceptance into the group really does little for your self-esteem.

Still, despite these possible disadvantages, most teens want to be included in some group. One fifteen-year-old explains: "Since I've moved here, I've tried my hardest. Sometimes I just have to walk away and stick to myself and cry a lot to my mom."

Kids who have never felt like an outsider or who are outgoing often don't realize the struggle that goes on inside a shy person trying to break into a new setting. Michelle says: "I feel that if a person is an outsider, it is because he chooses to be that way."

The overwhelming majority of respondents on the high school survey, however, disagree. Typical of the comments was this one from Bobbie, 15: "I just moved here and I feel very lonely and hurt. I'm confused right now, and I'm trying to make friends, but everyone has their little groups. I'm still working on how to handle this situation." Even a foreign exchange student, who generally has the support of the school and enjoys more than the usual attention afforded to newcomers, explains: "When I came to the United States, I was first an outsider to my host family, then in school. The language was quite difficult. I finally had to join clubs to get to know people."

If you feel like an outsider, it may help to remember that not belonging to a group isn't always personal rejection. If you were to examine the real underlying feelings of the group members, you might find that they're just not in the market for *any* new friends. They could be satisfied with the people they already have. Your personality has nothing to do with their ignoring you.

That is not to say that you can't work your way into the group, just that it *will* definitely take work. Perhaps you might decide that being in a particular group is not worth the effort. Betty, 18, came to that conclusion: "At my school, you're either popular or you're nothing. That's especially true in the junior high here, I think, because then it really matters to you. By the time you're a junior or senior, it really doesn't matter that much anymore. I never did work my way into one particular group. I probably could have if I had really wanted to that badly, but after a while they all seemed so money crazy and unreal."

Girls, particularly, may have trouble with groups, says researcher Janet Lever. When girls are younger, they usually play games like jacks, house, turning cartwheels—activities that require only one or two close friends. Boys, on the other hand, often play sports that involve getting along with many boys. As a result, boys develop more childhood skills in compromising and being accepted into a group than most girls do.

TIPS FOR OUTSIDERS MOVING IN

1. Get to know people one on one. "All my life I've been 'the new kid in town.' I'm an army brat and have moved a million times. When I was younger, it never was a problem because I just sort of blended into the group. Now it's a little more difficult. I usually get into a club or team and find one person who is nice to me there. Through them, I meet their friends and branch out." Overwhelmingly, this was the most frequently given advice from kids who have moved a lot. Meet people one at a time and then they will gradually introduce you to their friends. And

pay particular attention to others who seem to be
on the fringes of a group, because they will probably welcome your approach more than the group
leaders.

2. *Join groups with interests or skills
that you enjoy.* "When I moved here three years
ago, I got into football. At first they just didn't
notice me, but I really started trying to do good—
trying to impress them on the field. Finally, I got
their attention and I started meeting people," Ron
recalls. Baseball player Jeff agrees: "I was an outsider the first year I played baseball for the
school. The older guys wouldn't accept me. Finally, though, they accepted me for my ability,
then as a person."

If you're not interested in sports, try other activities: "I was transferred onto the Silverados by my
own drill team, where I met a lot of people. None of
them are close yet, but I'm getting there," Janet
explains. Rhonda says, "For me, it was band. I had a
very close friendship with a girl in junior high.
When we went to high school, she started hanging around with the other band members and introduced them to me. After about a year, I felt
comfortable and welcome in their group."
Fifteen-year-old Craig says his church group
made the difference: "At first people thought I
was stuck up, and that really upset me. But I got
in with a church youth group and now they know
me. They respect me."

3. *Talk to people, be friendly, be open.*
"You have to socialize with people to get to know

their ways," advises Bob. "Get involved by making a point to talk to people wherever you meet them. I used to sit back and wait until someone said 'hi' to me. Then after a while, I started introducing myself to other people. This is one of the hardest things to do, but you have to." Myra agrees: "One day I got tired of being insecure and unnoticed. I knew I was an all right person, so I started speaking up. Now I feel better." Bart advises that you start talking with little things—like asking to borrow a pencil or asking about class rules.

Several teens also feel that you have to be willing to talk about yourself. "You have to show them yourself, tell them stories about yourself, give them your ideas and opinions," says Bob. "They have to know what I feel to appreciate me. Everyone wants to know how you react in certain situations."

4. *Take initiative in inviting people places and calling them on the phone.* Brenda, 16, recalls, "I offered one of the girls a ride home from school one day. The next day she introduced me to a lot of the people she knew." Charece remembers, "I got to know one guy who asked me out. Then after I got to meet some of his friends, I started to invite people to do things with me." Steve adds, "I just tried to get to know a couple of kids who sat next to me in class and then I started calling them up to talk at home. Finally, I asked them to go someplace and that was the beginning of a good relationship."

5. *Go to work helping someone.* "When I moved here last year, I joined Young Life and a church and started to work," Dave says. Bonnie agrees with his philosophy: "I always feel like an outsider when I join something new. I try to do something for the club or team. Make the posters no one else wants to make. Sell the most magazine subscriptions. Just something."

Finally, keep in mind that working your way into a group involves being true to yourself and investing time. Carrie says, "I've moved around lots of times. You just have to be yourself and you find people who will accept you the way you are and take you for what you are." Don sums up: "It takes time—you can't just jump to the top of the ladder, you have to climb it."

PARTIES

How to Be a Welcome Party-Goer.

Sooner or later, that first party invitation will come. If you're nervous at a party or with a new group informally, you certainly can't count on your brain to come up with the should's and should not's on the spur of the moment. The following are some suggestions for making party-going easier:

Hosts and hostesses want you to fit into their party as much as you want to fit in yourself. Begin by asking whoever invited you any questions you may have about what to wear, who else will be there, what is going to happen. At the time of the invitation you might say something like, "You said we were going to be swimming—should I wear a suit and coverup or will there be a place to change there?" Usually, any question whatsoever about appropriate dress will bring an explanation about what activities are planned for the evening. Listen. That way you can fill in between the lines and make some decisions for yourself.

You can also ask who else is coming (after you've already accepted the invitation, of course), so that you can make arrangements to come with another guest or so that you can have topics of conversation in mind for specific people.

Second, don't arrive too early or too late. Ask other people who are going to the party what time they're planning to be there. Although your host may have given you a general time like "after the football game," someone else can explain specifically: "It'll probably be 10:30 before everybody gets there because most of those coming are in the band and they'll have to change from their uniforms first." When you arrive too early, you often delay the hostess' preparation and find yourself in the way. He or she is torn between entertaining you and dishing up the dip and chips for the table. And if you arrive too late, you may miss the initial warm-up conversations and introductions and find yourself out of step for the whole evening.

Third, amuse yourself and don't wait to be entertained or plugged into the group. If you're shy or find yourself at a party where you don't know many people, stay busy. Offer to select and play the records. Replenish the candy dish. Show other people coming in where to put coats or get Cokes.

Of course, if none of the above "chores" brings you into conversation with anyone, you'll have to be more forward and approach someone to talk. Choose someone who looks like he's not much a part of the group, rather than someone who is in the middle of things, and begin a conversation as I've mentioned in Chapter 2.

If you can't think of anything specific to say about what's going on, just say that you feel shy because you don't know anybody. Most people will feel sympathetic and will meet you more than halfway. Plaster an alert, friendly, I-want-to-be-included look on your face and people will respond.

Introductions when you enter a group shouldn't be too formal. Save yourself and others some embarrassment, though, if you think they don't remember you by mentioning your name again. For instance, you could say, "I'm Nita, remember? From last weekend with Donna and Al at the Pizza Hut?" Just a little jog of their memory takes people off the hook about not remembering where they know you from.

Once you get into the group, speak up early in the conversation. The longer you just stand and listen, the harder it becomes to say anything. You keep thinking that when you do make your entry, it had better be something smashingly witty. And nothing running through your mind quite measures up. If you wait until everyone else gives an opinion about something, chances are you will either have to contradict or repeat what someone else has just said. Either way, you'll probably think it's easier to keep your mouth shut and you'll end the conversation feeling like a bump on a pickle.

To keep a conversation going once you find yourself in the group, have some topics in mind to throw out for informal opinions: "Did you hear about the wreck on Jones Road yesterday? Do you know if anyone was injured?" Or, "Somebody told me last week that we'd already lost too many games to be in the running for District. Does anybody know if that's right?"

In other words, you're throwing out a topic that almost everyone in the group can talk about —correctly or incorrectly—but that's secondary to your purpose at the moment. If nobody responds, catch the eye of a single individual and he or she will generally answer or comment to lead the conversation further.

One last thing about being a part of a conversational group—don't just leave. If you haven't contributed much to the conversation, you might be tempted to just "fade" away into the scenery and not call attention to your leaving. But you should always say something to excuse yourself: "Oh, there's Margie; I've got to go ask her something."

Or, "I think I'll go get another piece of cake." A departure statement lets people know that you feel enough a part of the group to explain when you leave. When you just disappear, people may think you are offended in some way or that you don't consider yourself part of them. Finally, when you're leaving a party for good, be specific about saying thank you. "I had a nice time; thanks for inviting me" is a holdover from your mother's instructions about your first birthday party. Now that you're older, you'll want the "thank you" to sound more sincere than just good manners. Comment on one or two specific things you enjoyed: "Thanks for inviting me; I sure hope your mom serves the same kind of avocado dip next time," said teasingly. Or, "This was really fun; I haven't laughed so hard all year." A sincere compliment leaves a pleasant glow to last the host/hostess through the cleanup.

How to Be a Good Party-Giver.

In a nutshell, be all things to all people. You call the show for this particular evening, and ultimately you are responsible for seeing that your guests have a good time. If that's not your interest, perhaps you'd better forget giving a party and plan to get together with your friends to see a movie or go out for Chinese food.

That is not to say you shouldn't and can't enjoy your own parties, but just that you need to keep your guests' good time foremost in your mind. Here are some tips to help you do that:

1. *Stay visible.* Sometimes the host or hostess gets so involved in a closed conversation or activity with special best friends, he or she forgets about other guests. A party is not the time to indulge yourself in a heart-to-heart discussion about your boyfriend problem. Try to devote a few minutes of conversation to each guest and make him or her feel special to you.

Always greet each person when he arrives and go to the door with him to say good-bye when he leaves. When you're intensely involved in a game of Hearts at the dining room table and someone waves that he is leaving, don't just wave back and continue with your game. You're telling him that his presence or lack of it doesn't really matter to you. If you liked him enough to invite him, don't spoil the evening for him by ignoring his leaving.

2. *Make sure that all your guests know each other and try to draw shy kids into conversations.* Sometimes you'll find that this can best be accomplished with warm-up topics you can throw out when the first few people arrive. For instance, "Joel, did you tell them about what Mr. Decker said about the cafeteria fight?" Joel can then take the floor.

It also helps to have last-minute busy work to give shy guests something to do. For instance, ask early arrivals to set up the Ping-Pong table and net. Or, you can have them sort out the two decks of cards still mixed together from last time you used them. These kinds of projects give shy people something to do besides feel awkward and provide them with a topic of conversation. Don't take it for granted that because you know all the kids, they all know each other. Make introductions. Especially, introduce your friends to your parents or any other adults helping with the party. In general, the rule books say to introduce men to women and young people to older people: "Sherrie, this is Mike," Or, "Daddy, this is Stephanie."

Another tip to make it easier for your guests when they are introduced: Add a comment that will help them begin talking. For instance, "Daddy, this is Stephanie. She's on the volleyball team." That gives Daddy a clue about what to say to her. Or, "Sherrie, this is Mike. He and I suffer through chemistry together." Mike can then follow up with a comment about how boring chemistry is or ask Sherrie if she's had the course.

3. *Handle troublemakers.* Don't allow some guests to make others uncomfortable by insisting they join in an activity when they seem reluctant. If Sara and three of her friends suggest that everybody leave to go "wrap" a neighbor's house, say that you don't think everybody else wants to. In other words, be the "wet blanket" yourself rather than make other guests feel uncomfortable.

Occasionally you will find yourself host or hostess when two of your guests don't get along. If they get into an argument and get loud so that you and the others can't ignore what's going on, say something like, "Come on, you two, you're making the rest of us feel uncomfortable." Such a statement puts them on the spot before the others. They will either drop the subject or leave, and you're no longer responsible.

4. Be gracious about accidents. Kathi relates one such incident: "I threw up at a party on someone's couch. I was extremely embarrassed because I really was sick. I ate too many M & M's. Everyone asked me if I was okay, and that made me feel much better."

When someone scratches your favorite record or turns over his drink on the carpet, try to help him through his embarrassment. Humor helps— although not humor at your guest's expense. For instance, with a broken record you might say, "Well, I bet old Kenny Rogers really has a scratchy voice now."

If a similar accident has happened to you, relate that to the guest and make him feel like he's not a freak. Accept an apology for any such accident, try to change the subject as soon as possible, and direct attention away from whatever happened. Your guest will be eternally grateful for such thoughtfulness.

You as a host or hostess set the tone for your party. Long after the chips are gone and the jokes are old, your guests will remember a warm, welcome atmosphere.

SOCIAL BLUNDERS

One last thing about fitting into a group. Unless you're one of the rare, perfect specimens of humanity on the planet, you will occasionally make social blunders like the following made by teens responding to the survey:

- I was out one night with some friends and the guy I liked, and we stopped at a store to get some gum. We were in a hurry so Pam and I jumped out of the car and were running up to the door. Well, all of a sudden, I tripped up the curb and rolled over and landed on my bottom! I was so embarrassed because the boy I wanted to date was in the car watching. Everyone was laughing so hard and despite everything, he still asked me out.
- I sing in the school choir, and every year we go to a contest where you sing a solo in front of a judge. Before I was supposed to sing, I was helping a friend with his solo, going over and over the words with him. When my turn was called—after I'd practiced six weeks for my solo—I started to sing the friend's song.
- My boyfriend and I went to a nice restaurant and I dumped a plate of spaghetti all over the person sitting across the aisle from me. I screamed and the other person jumped and everybody at the whole restaurant started laughing.

- I was walking down the hall and my friend said John was behind us. Well, I misunderstood what my friend said and I just thought he mentioned John's name—not that he was actually behind us. I started saying how dumb John was and that he was the kind of kid who would trip on his own feet and then look down and say "dumb shoes." Well, when we turned the corner, my friend grabbed me and told me that John had been walking right behind us. I haven't had the guts to talk to him since.
- I was telling this group that I didn't like one kind of class ring and then I noticed that this girl in the group had on the exact kind of ring I was describing.
- I was visiting a friend of mine in Michigan and they'd just bought some new property. While they were gone one Saturday morning, I thought I'd just help out by pulling weeds in the yard. Well, what I thought were weeds happened to be tiny trees he'd planted on his daughter's birthday.
- I wore nice dress clothes to the homecoming last year and I really felt dumb because no one here dresses up like that—I found out later.
- I spilled Kool-Aid all over a friend's carpet.
- I was writing a note in a girl's yearbook. My mind just went blank. I stood there looking at her and couldn't even think of her name. I had to ask her.

If you've committed similar blunders, try to

remember that you're not the only dumb, clumsy, or tactless teen in the world.

How do you overcome such blunders and regain your composure?

If you fall, get up quickly and try a little humor. Although most people will laugh because anyone who takes an unexpected tumble looks funny, they are not laughing *at* you but *with* you—provided you laugh. I feel safe in assuming that everyone on the planet who walks upright has taken at least one embarrassing fall in his or her life. Rise and shine is the best policy.

After a tactless statement, try an honest apology. Say that you're sorry, that you were wrong, that you sometimes make snap judgments, or that you weren't thinking. People respect an honest apology and are more forgiving than you might think. Or, again, you might try humor. Say something like, "I'm known around here for my big mouth and little brain." Or, "Your turn, you want to punch me out now or later?"

If dress seems to be the problem, a good rule-of-thumb is to be conservative rather than overdressed. When in doubt, don't. But once you arrive in the wrong outfit, grin and bear it with as little fuss as possible. If you don't make a big deal about it, others won't either.

If you break, damage, or lose something, apologize and then replace it the next day with a duplicate or something similar.

If you mess something up, clean it up.

When you goof in any of these ways, be as

thoughtful as possible in the aftermath and then suffer in silence. Remember that no one is goof-proof. Politicians gesturing to their audiences knock over microphones; models trip on the walkways; comedians botch their punchlines.

Eventually, the laughter will die down, your face will regain its natural color, and life will go on. Your attitude is the key to walking into and away from groups a winner.

Chapter Four
DATING DYNAMICS

SOONER OR LATER most teens develop special feelings for one particular girl or guy—feelings that are different from those they have for their other friends.

You ask for an extra house key, a ride to the dance with an older brother and his date, a bigger allowance, permission for a part-time job, and later curfew. You're ready for the BIG game—until you look in the mirror and have second thoughts.

APPEARANCE ISN'T DESTINY

"Who would go out with someone who looks like me?" reverberates around the curves of many minds and stands in the way of attempts to develop dating relationships.

Granted, attractiveness opens doors. In a recent

study at the University of Minnesota, males and females whose telephone conversations were recorded were told they were talking to either an attractive or unattractive person. The taped conversations were later evaluated by judges who were unaware of what each caller had been told about attractiveness. The males who thought they were talking to attractive females judged them to be more poised, more sociable, and more vivacious. Females who thought they were talking to good-looking males judged them to be more sociable, interesting, independent, outgoing, and humorous.

And many other researchers have gathered similar results: Attractive people are thought to be more genuine, sincere, warm, modest, sensitive, interesting, strong, exciting, and of better character than the less attractive. They get better grades, more attention, higher-paying jobs.

But, appearance isn't destiny.

Studies also show that intelligence, sex, and height determine your chances and choices to a large degree. Although you're career chances are better if you're born male, I know lots of successful businesswomen. And although in our society tall seems to be better than short, I've known a lot of short successful people.

I repeat, a less-than-perfect face or body won't handicap you. Sophia Loren's mouth is too large; Farrah Fawcett's jaw is square; Sandy Duncan has a false eye; Barbra Streisand has a crooked nose; Prince Charles has big ears; John Travolta has a long, pointed chin.

The most important thing about your appearance is how *you* feel about it. Whether you think you're good-looking or ugly can influence your personality—drastically. When you feel attractive, you usually are friendly, talkative, poised, and can show interest in others. When you feel ugly, you frown, show a sour disposition, feel self-conscious, talk less, and avoid others. As Dale Carnegie says in his book *How to Win Friends and Influence People,* " . . . the expression a woman wears on her face is far more important than the clothes she wears on her back."

Does that mean that you should not care how you look? Of course not. Attractiveness counts. But attractiveness involves much more than face, figure, stature. Accept the things about your appearance that you can't change, and learn to package yourself in appealing wrap and ribbons.

First, pay attention to proper diet and exercise. If you need to gain weight, try to increase your stomach capacity by eating more frequently. Add the extras, such as butter and gravies and sauces to your foods. Also, exercise increases your appetite.

If you need to lose weight, follow a sensible diet that includes food from the four food groups and adhere to the number of calories your body requires per day. Males between 13 and 19 need between 3,100–3,600 calories daily; females 13 to

19 need between 2,400–2,600 calories daily. To burn off one pound of body fat, you must cut your diet by 3,500 calories—and cut slowly. Losing 2 to 3 pounds per week is safe, and the pounds are easier to keep off than fast weight losses. The secret to fad diets is that they bore you to death and you automatically eat less—you get tired of all bananas, avocados, tossed salad, or salted peanuts. Increasing exercise (firm beats flabby) and cutting calories are the most sensible and effective ways to have a nice figure.

Second, acne is a problem for many teens. Although you can't cure acne caused by heredity, you can control acne caused by medicines, cosmetics, dirt, and stress. Recent studies show that over-the-counter medicines that contain bromides, cortisones, and iodines *may* cause acne. If it's necessary to take medicines, ask your doctor about your choices. Cosmetics that have an oil base can aggravate complexion problems, but light makeup with a water base will *not* clog pores and can cover problems effectively.

Your best defense against complexion problems is cleanliness. Adolescent skin frequently is oily, and oily skin attracts dirt. Cleanse often with strong soaps, alcoholic fresheners, and medicated lotions. Keep stray oily hair off your face.

Third, hair care is important to overall appearance. Keep your hair clean and neat with stylish cuts that are suitable for your face shape. Save your money and go to a stylist who can suggest hairstyles to suit your lifestyle and personality.

Avoid harming your hair by excessive use of dryers and hot curlers and by excessive pulling and tension when curling, brushing, combing, and pinning. Proper diet also contributes to healthy, shiny hair.

Finally, pay attention to your clothes. Fashion-conscious, well-dressed teens stress investing in better, but fewer clothes. If you have a limited budget, you have to shop harder. Remember the two most important elements of your overall dress—line and color. Horizontal lines make you look shorter and wider, while vertical lines make you look taller and slimmer.

Pay particular attention to color coordination. When you put colors together, stay within tonal families to be safe. Striking contrasts work sometimes—and sometimes they don't.

Most importantly, choose a proper fit. Frequently, overweight people choose tight clothing, thinking it makes them look smaller. Actually, the opposite is true. Tight clothes reveal all the bulges and draw attention to figure flaws. If in doubt about color and fit, ask a salesclerk for help or trust a friend whose clothing you admire. And, of course, it goes without saying that clothes should be clean and in good repair—no missing buttons or rips.

Good grooming (diet, exercise, skin and hair care, clothing) picks up where Mother Nature left off. Packaging yourself well makes you feel good about yourself. And when you feel self-confident, you can show interest in other people.

DOS AND DON'TS OF DATE INVITATIONS

Okay, so you're convinced that attractiveness involves more than a nose job. The next question is how to approach that special person for a date and a chance to get to know him or her more intimately.

Avoid cutesy lines. Chris Cleinke, a psychologist who has written a book called *First Impressions*, finds in his research that females prefer a casual comment or direct question rather than a cutesy opener. Not having to charm a girl in the first few words to make a date should be a relief to millions of guys trying to memorize witty come-ons. First of all, get to know the person you want to date through conversation. Check some of the suggestions in Chapter 2 for openers with a stranger, acquaintance, or casual friend.

Many teens find it easier to ask for a date on the telephone because they don't have to worry about body language or privacy or interruptions. If you choose to phone, call at a convenient time. Just because your family always eats dinner at exactly 6:00, that doesn't mean everyone does. Try to avoid calling near any mealtime or late at night. There's no sense in the girl's family having two strikes against you before she ever says "yes."

When you answer the phone, try to use a pleasant voice. Some people sound like they're smiling and happy you called. Others answer with a why-did-you-bother-me-in-the-middle-of-my-favorite-TV-program tone.

When you phone, don't play "guess who?" That's a juvenile game that should end in fourth grade. If he or she guesses eight other names before yours, it certainly doesn't do much for your ego. And most of the time, the other person is embarrassed by being put on the spot.

If you're planning to ask out someone who may not remember you well, make an initial contact by phone or in person. You could call about a specific class assignment or other information about school. Or, ask advice about a fund-raising project or tell some news about a mutual friend. Then when you follow up that call in a few days, he or she will have you in mind.

Another warm-up idea is to invite the person to go along on a group activity: "A bunch of us are going to go to the beach Saturday. Do you want to come along?" Group dates are much easier to handle for the first few times than single dates because you can depend on others to carry the conversation and create a fun atmosphere.

When you do ask for a one-to-one date, get to the point and be specific. Always have tentative plans and alternate suggestions in case the first choice doesn't work out. For instance, "I was wondering if you'd like to go to a movie with me Friday night. I thought we could see. . ." If she says that she's seen that movie, either suggest another one or ask her if she has a particular movie she'd like to see. If she turns down the second movie and doesn't have another suggestion, listen carefully to any explanation she offers. If she says she can't go because she has to babysit, use your alternate plan—would she like to go ice-skating Saturday afternoon? Note the change of day and time. Her answer to the second invitation should definitely let you know whether she's interested in going out with you at all.

If she says yes, plan the specifics together—what time the movie begins and what time you should pick her up. Give your date some choice (for instance, what movie to see or if she prefers Italian or Chinese food), but be ready with specific suggestions. The date has no way of knowing how much money you have to spend and how far you want to drive across town.

If she says no because she has other plans or other legitimate reasons, tell her you'll call again about something else for next weekend. If, however, you can tell that she just doesn't want to go out with you, end the conversation politely.

She may turn you down for any number of good reasons. She may feel sick. She may be worried over a personal problem like a death in the family or a big fight between her parents. She may be embarrassed about her address and not want you to pick her up. She may not have money to buy new clothes for the dance. She may be excessively shy or she may be embarrassed to admit her parents won't let her date. (This happens more frequently than you realize.)

Whatever the reason for the turndown, end the conversation by saying that you're sorry she can't make it, that maybe you'll be able to get together some other time, or that you'll see her in school. If the girl has sounded cold and untalkative when you phone, keep in mind that her silence may be due to lack of privacy on the other end.

When you find yourself in the position of turning down a date, do so with utmost care—you're dealing with someone's shaky ego. You don't need to lie or offer elaborate explanations about why you don't want to go out, but you don't have to be cruel either.

If, on the other hand, you'd like to go out with the person, but you just don't want to go where he or she has suggested or you have a time conflict, by all means let the person know that. He or she will be relieved if you offer an explanation or alternate suggestion.

The overriding concern is not to be unfeeling. Some teens interpret that to mean never giving a definite "no," and they continue to lead the other person on. A courteous but firm, "No, I don't think so, but thank you for inviting me," is far better than a lame excuse every time the caller risks his or her ego again.

COMMUNICATION BETWEEN THE SEXES

Because most dating relationships grow out of friendship, most teens expect the same qualities in their dates as in their close friends—honesty, loyalty, openness, and trust.

Honesty in a dating relationship means being

up-front with your intentions. Honesty means you don't ask for or accept dates for a free concert ticket, popularity with the "right" group, or help for an upcoming math test. If you're ashamed to admit your motives, perhaps the date is not a good idea in the first place.

Honesty also invites sending clear signals where sex is concerned. In our society a girl is trained to be pleased when a male makes a pass at her. Gloria Steinem calls this the "man junkie" syndrome, the need to gain self-esteem from the attention of the opposite sex. If this is the case, a girl may tease by the way she sits, stands, walks, dresses, smiles, talks, jokes, hugs, and kisses "just friends." But once she knows that the boy finds her attractive, she is satisfied. The game is over— for her.

But not necessarily for the boy. He may not always understand that the girl's flirting is just a game, that she means to go no further. When she stops his sexual advances, he often feels resentful and tricked. Of course, a boy may read signals incorrectly or may pick up signals when they don't exist because society has conditioned him, too, to act macho toward females. He is told that girls don't always mean "no" when they say it. He learns that "no" may be a face-saving ploy when a girl really means "maybe," or "I'll think about it," or even "yes." He may also interpret constant flirting with other males as evidence that she is free with her sexual favors to everyone. He may even think she *expects* an advance from him, or that all males are supposed to be super go-getters on dates, or that she will think he's weird if he doesn't try something. He may even have the ridiculous idea that the girl should pay him for the date with sex. Whatever your feelings about sexual relationships, you must communicate clearly how you feel. And once you set your limits in the area of sex, try to protect your date's ego. Say that you don't invite anyone into your house when your parents aren't home, or you don't usually take a girl to the beach alone. Selfish sex games and manipulation can be far too destructive to a teen's personality development.

Openness is a second quality that rates high on the date list. When you share ideas, dreams, opinions, and values, you are sharing part of yourself. To make the relationship all it can be, both people have to open up to the same extent. Just as with any other close friend, you shouldn't have to "slide" over hurt feelings and hide your pain. You shouldn't have to be uncomfortable to make the other person comfortable. A loving relationship can continue to grow only as both partners participate in the give-and-take equally. If all the giving is one-sided, sooner or later someone will explode with resentment.

Such was the case with Jeff and Susan, who had been dating steadily all through their sophomore and junior years. One Saturday night, without warning, Jeff said simply that he thought they should break it off. No new girl, no complaints, no explanations. Perhaps he didn't even know at the time specifically why his feelings for Susan had disappeared. But later in a conversation with his best friend, he aired some of their problems.

Susan had always chosen the places they went with little regard for what Jeff wanted to do. He liked rodeos and she frequently teased him when he mentioned that they go to one. Instead, she preferred movies and going out to dinner. And when they were with a group of their friends, Jeff felt that she ignored him and frequently flirted with other guys just to make him jealous. Jeff's main interest was horses, particularly the two he was grooming for shows. Susan never asked him about them and, he said, acted like she was bored when the subject came up. So, he always talked about what she was interested in.

Certainly, in their case, Susan showed insensitivity, but Jeff, too, was at fault for not speaking up about how he felt all along rather than letting his resentment build until it destroyed the relationship.

Openness can ease a multitude of potential problems.

Finally, openness necessitates loyalty. Because of the nature of a dating relationship and the closeness that develops when two teens share intimate problems and feelings, loyalty becomes the epitome of respect. The better you know someone, the deeper you can hurt them. It's as if they have locked all their valuables in your safe-deposit box. To be truly open, a partner must feel that if and when your relationship ends, you will be the kind of person who will throw away the key.

If you yield to the temptation to gossip, it affects your own self-respect. And nothing lowers you in the eyes of former partners or mutual friends more than your gossiping about things told to you in confidence.

Honesty, openness, loyalty—they go hand in hand to take you from the first-date jitters to a meaningful relationship.

WHAT HAPPENS WHEN THE FLAME GOES OUT?

Is it possible to be "just friends" with an ex-boyfriend or girlfriend? Psychologists disagree. So do teens. Twenty-five percent of the boys and twenty-four percent of the girls in the high school survey said absolutely not.

> • No, they can't be friends. I've been going with the same guy for three years and so much went on between us, it's impossible. Too many feelings are in that gap—maybe if we weren't so close or if it didn't hurt so much.
>
> • No, because once you break up with her, you don't really ever want to see her anymore.
>
> • I personally cannot be just friends with an ex-girlfriend because even after we break up, I always still have feelings, because I usually get very involved.
>
> • No, I'd like to be but things never work out. You almost ignore each other. You either feel uneasy or guilty or something. I'd love

to be friends with an "ex" but it's never the same.

Seventy-five percent of the boys and seventy-six percent of the girls, however, disagree, saying that being "just friends" is possible.

- Yes, if you know so much about them, you should at least keep the friendship.

- Yes, it's so much easier that way! Then you can even hold on to your memories.

- A deeper bond than "just friends" has already been made, but it has probably been just frayed instead of truly broken.

- Yes, if you used to be together, then you must still have a lot in common and things to talk about.

- Yes, I think you can, because my mother and father are divorced now and they are better friends than they have ever been. So I think the same goes with girlfriends or boyfriends.

Although the big majority said "just friends" is possible, most qualify their "yes," pointing out that the "after" relationship depends on how close the couple was to begin with, the personality of the two people involved, and the time lapse.

- Yes, you can be friends. In fact I am in better perspective with my ex-boyfriend. He's a great friend and a more understanding person because of the break-up. But one thing you must remember—it takes TIME to get a relationship back together.

- Yes, you can if you don't hold grudges.
- Yes, you can once you both have other girlfriends and boyfriends.
- Yes, you can in rare cases. But usually, the same problems that broke you up will continue to surface and interfere with your friendship.
- Yes, I've always stayed real close to my ex-boyfriends. I feel that I am mature enough to clear all conflicts with my ex-boyfriends before we break up. I hope I never lose a friendship over a dating problem.
- It takes a lot of willpower on both people's part. You never know when the "other" relationship might begin again and you have to have the courage to stop it.
- Yes, but it's very difficult because they know a lot about you and you can't talk about many things to them anymore.

To sum up the "yes," "no," and "it depends" answers: If you have a casual, friendly dating relationship to begin with, you should be able to remain friends after a break-up. But if you have a serious, long-term dating relationship, being just friends proves much more difficult. But mature, forgiving, caring personalities, along with time, can help rework the relationship into friendship again.

Despite the potential for pain, dating leads you to examine and evaluate your own goals, ideas, values, and opinions. Show genuine interest in the other person, and he or she will find you attractive. Most of all, don't forget common courtesy and sensitivity in asking for and turning down dates.

Once a dating relationship has begun, keep the lines of communication open. Dating provides the basis for probably the most serious adult commitment you will make, marriage. And the lasting love that grows into marriage doesn't just zap you—it grows from friendship. So choose dates as carefully as best friends.

Chapter Five

WHEN FRIENDSHIP HURTS

CAN CLOSE FRIENDS ever be too close?
Has a friend ever misused you? Have you ever
felt betrayed? These questions put to the survey
group of high schoolers revealed some very common friendship problems. Some teens said they
had been able to work out the problems and to
develop an ever better friendship than before.
Others said they had continued in the relationship but really didn't trust this friend as before.
Many considered their relationship beyond repair.

How do you decide when a friendship has become harmful? How do you clear the air effectively with a friend without ending the relationship? If necessary, how can you end a friendship
without hard feelings? Let's take the answers to
these questions one at a time.

COMPETITION AND JEALOUSY

Friends often find themselves envious or envied about money, accomplishments, or popularity. Carol, 16, says: "I had a best friend who got to know the popular girls and they accepted her into their group and she blew me off. She would harass me at school and at home. I hated her."

Particularly serious problems develop when the competition involves a boyfriend or girlfriend situation. Judy confides: "A friend of mine found out I liked a certain boy, and she started flirting with him and following him around, and she really didn't even like him. This was heartbreaking to me because I could not believe that a friend of mine would do that to me."

Several guys had similar complaints about best friends competing for their girlfriends and even taking the girlfriends out when they were out of town.

In such situations of competition and jealousy, problems develop from both sides. The friend who "outshines" may feel guilty and try to stifle his own abilities, and therefore be unable to feel close to the old friend again. Another may flaunt his or her accomplishments and make the friend feel less important in the relationship. But sometimes the hurt results from the loser's outlook. The person who has "come in second" sometimes imagines that the winning friend has become a snob and looks down on him or her, thus making it hard for the friend to keep the relationship on the same course as before. The "second best" may show resentment and continually put himself down and point out his own weaknesses, making the other friend feel guilty.

This is not to say that all competition is bad. Two friends who are both competitive in basketball can keep each other's skills at optimum level—working to outdo the other makes both better players. Rather than kill a relationship, healthy competition can add spice. Penny remarks: "My friends have to be on the same or on a higher level than me. It sounds cruel, but my friends have to be smart, because I like competition. I don't want friends who admire me."

Only when one friend *always* outdistances the other will there be trouble. Because competition is one of the harder problems to overcome in a relationship, most people tend to choose friends they consider their equals.

POSSESSIVENESS

"The condition which high friendship demands is ability to do without it," says essayist Emerson. People who give the impression that they must have a certain friendship to survive often frighten the would-be friend away. Coming on too strongly too soon may make you a burden.

Some teens feel that friends who are too possessive limit their privacy.

• They don't give you any space.

- Sometimes close friends pry into your affairs that you don't want to even tell anyone.
- I have a friend who's always asking "what's wrong?" when I really don't want to discuss it. I hate that.

Other teens feel that possessive friends cheat them of time they'd like to spend with family or other friends:

- When your close friends start acting possessive toward you, like getting jealous if you go out with other friends, spend the night with someone else, etc., that's a little too close.
- When they get too close, they ignore other people, making others not like them or me either.
- I have a close friend who wants me to do *everything* with her and she just assumes I'll agree. She doesn't give me any freedom.
- I have a good friend who wants to be around all the time. It would be okay sometimes, but I have other friends and my family who I like to do things with. She is trying to, or has been trying to, break up a friendship I have with a guy, and with another best friend, so she can be closer to me.

Another reason possessive friendships can be harmful involves the predicaments of one or both when the friendship breaks up:

- My very best friend and I are too close. I

say this because over the years we became so dependent that now in our senior year, she has had to move and we are both finding it hard to function.

•I broke off my relationship totally with one girl because I was becoming too dependent on her and people started noticing and telling me so. I don't ever want to be that dependent again.

Smothering friendships also blur the line of individuality:

•I became too close with my friend and it never caused problems until we separated last year. Everything was "we this" and "we that"; we both miss each other a great deal. I'm just now getting my own self-image.

•I have a friend who doesn't even like herself anymore. She tries to act like me.

Finally, a too-close friendship can simply bore you to death:

•I get tired of always knowing what she'll do. There has to be some mystery about a person.

• You spend too much time together and you start to get on each other's nerves and tend to get into arguments easier, which leads to hatred! Not a good way to end a friendship.

Of course, the problem of possessiveness in a relationship is not always on the side of the person who is trying to possess the other's time and energy. Sometimes friends encourage overdependence on themselves to build their own egos. They often tell themselves that they are helping the dependent friend, but actually more often they are keeping the person helpless and not allowing him or her to learn self-reliance.

Other relationships and time spent away from each other enrich a friendship and make both people more interesting. A possessive relationship is like a fire without oxygen. It goes out.

CRITICISM

Accepting criticism from a friend has much to do with why and how—the person's motives and manner. Rather than feeling hurt by something a friend says or does carelessly, always give the friend the benefit of the doubt. Assume he doesn't mean to hurt you. Of course, when the criticism is stated outright, then try to weigh the friend's motives. Is he or she trying to hurt you or to improve you?

At first, it's natural to respond to criticism with anger, but the mark of a true friend with sincere motives is his ability to hold on until your anger subsides so that you can face the real issue with an open mind. If you approach the critical remark positively, you'll often find that the criticism may do you much more good than praise. Most people are aware of their own good points. It's the weaknesses that keep us blindfolded.

If after you have faced criticism openly and

think your friend's motives are appropriate and helpful, ask for a specific solution or suggestion to correct the problem. Working out a solution to improve your character is a freedom few friends afford each other. Such liberties cement friendships closer than total admiration ever can.

But not all criticism can be turned to profit. Don't let a friend's critical attitude and remarks destroy you as a person. This may happen even when the friend's motive is to help you. Parents who think they are helping a teen to improve often nag him to the point that his self-esteem wilts. Friends can be guilty of the same thing—criticizing you to help you improve until you reach a point of despair about your own abilities and character.

And of course, sometimes you may decide a friendship is parasitic—a friend builds herself up by tearing you down. This type of friendship has no redeeming value and is the kind you need to end immediately.

When can friendships stand "the truth"? When a friend's motive is to make you a better person and when he or she criticizes specific, correctable flaws rather than you as a person.

DRAINERS

Teens, particularly, have intense crises that need immediate attention. Katie expresses her frustration this way: "When I ask a friend, Jane, if we can talk privately sometime, she says yes. Then when the time rolls around, she's always busy with other people. This really hurts me. She knows that I need to talk with her, but she socializes instead. It makes me wonder if she's worth it. Is she really a friend?"

Like Katie, many teens equate friendship with devotion to listening. And, granted, willingness to listen to problems is one of the things teens value most about their friendships.

But often talkers take advantage of listeners. They pour out their problems in such a steady, continuous stream that the listener feels emotionally drenched—as surely as if he'd been standing out in a heavy rain. Jill says: "I had a friend who liked to use me as a crutch and burden me down with all her problems and troubles to the point it would depress me. I slowly had to work my way away from her."

Another teen confides: "My mom died when I was thirteen. This friend's mother died last year, and she called me when she found out. I went over to her house to do what I could. This made me go through my mother's death all over again and kept me emotionally upset for a long time."

It's not that listeners don't care. For some, their own problems are just so heavy that they can't carry yours on their shoulders, too.

And even when a friend is able to shoulder the extra problems, dumping can be a sore spot when a friend blames you for bad advice. Another teen explains her frustration: "Kursten was always crying all over the place about how her dad wouldn't let her go out with this particular guy. She kept sneaking out to see him and then worrying that her dad would find out. She jumped every time the phone rang, thinking somebody was going to tell him. Finally, I got tired of hearing it and told her she should tell her dad what she was doing, apologize for doing it behind his back, and try to talk him into seeing the good points about Jimmy. Well, she did what I said, and it didn't work. She and her dad got into a bigger fight, and he grounded her from going anywhere for a month. Now she's blaming me."

Getting blamed for advice is a frequent complaint from teens who say their friendships are wearing thin. Being someone's scapegoat takes away whatever pleasure and satisfaction there may have been in helping the friend through troubled waters.

When you feel as though you've been through a rainstorm with a drainer—a storm which has left you exhausted and in "wet" spirits—you may have to pull away from that friend until both of you get your emotions all dried out.

CONFLICTING VALUES

Kids who choose to get involved in questionable behavior often need the courage of others to buoy them up. Researcher Denise Kandel found that after age, sex, and race, the most frequent criterion for choosing friends was deviant behavior, particularly the use of marijuana. In other words, teens who plan to sneak booze into the school dance, pass a teacher's grading key around before a final exam, or throw rocks through a window need friends to encourage them along.

Strong personalities can stand up to a friend's suggestion when they don't approve; weaker personalities can't. Matt, 16, says: "I have some friends that manipulate me into doing things that I don't think are right and that I don't really want to do. But if I'm going to be friends with them, what can I do?"

Weak personalities are not the only ones who have trouble in this area. Because some things are not absolutely right or wrong in every situation, morals can get blurred and friends can sometimes rationalize and make things look okay when you're with them. Only later do you feel that your own convictions have been violated.

Still other teens go along with compromising situations just to rebel against and hurt their parents. Joining in some activity that you feel is wrong just to spite your parents is like missing a party because you don't want to change shirts.

Teens usually resent parents' nagging them about friends who are a "bad influence," because they feel that their parents' objections imply that they are too weak to stand on their own values. Some teens zip up their minds and refuse to listen to any criticism about their choice of friends:

> • I just told my dad that the day he started hinting around about his dislike for one of my friends is the day I'm moving out.

- When my parents don't like one of my friends I just told them the good points about her and denied the bad things.
- I tell my parents that I don't pick their friends and they don't pick mine.

Other teens, like Lisa and Ken can step back and evaluate parental objections:

- My mother influences me tremendously about what friends I have without me even realizing it at the time. She casually and subtly talks negatively about the person until I'm convinced I don't want to be around the person anymore.
- I step back and take a look at both sides, then I decide.

Others, unable to admit that they may be wrong about a relationship, often feel compelled to forge ahead in the friendship, only to learn later that their parents were right:

- I didn't believe anything my parents said. I wouldn't listen or anything. I stuck up for my friend. But as it turns out—my parents were right.
- I went ahead and was friends with her even though my parents disapproved. But finally I wised up and saw her for the person she really was.
- I sort of buttered my parents up by saying, "Well, she makes straight As." I wanted to get my mom to like her, but I found out she

shouldn't have been friends with me after all.
• The way I handled the situation was by slowly getting out of the friendship. By the way—my mom has some intuition about things like that.

How do you feel about suppressing your own conscience and living by someone else's guidelines? Do your parents see conflict within you caused by a friendship? Are you compromising your own values just to express ill feelings toward your parents?

When you're caught in a friendship where you feel your friend is encouraging you to behave in a way you wouldn't on your own, do you count the cost? Is his or her acceptance worth losing your own self-respect and damaging your reputation with others?

TAKEN FOR GRANTED OR GRANITE

"I'm very into giving and it's like gasoline to a car. I need to give of myself and help others to run and live. But it's hard to judge how some will react," says fifteen-year-old Stephanie.

That's generosity and love. But more often than not, such friends are taken for granted and treated like granite. Another "giver" expresses her disappointment this way: "I'm a great 'helper,' I guess you would call me. I help many of my friends with problems and everything. People see me in that way. But I see myself a few times as depressed or lonely. I have friends but they seem like they don't help me when I need it."

Being generous out of your own free will gives satisfaction. But being exploited leaves quite another taste in your mouth:

> • One time when a friend invited me to Astroworld, she didn't find transportation and my mom ended up driving us. I felt angry because she always does that.
>
> • One friend and I had an entire four-day weekend planned, so I canceled all my other plans with my friends. Then she found out her boyfriend could go after all and it was all over for me. It wasn't that I was so mad about the weekend—it was just that she was inconsiderate enough to do it.

If you have a friend who seems to think of you as a piece of granite with no feelings and no desires except to please him or her, your friendship is probably building toward an explosion.

Don't ignore the feeling and the manipulation. Stand up to a dominating friend by simply stating how you feel. Say something like, "I don't feel right about what's happening between us. For the last four times, I've taken my car to the game. I feel like I'm paying more than my share."

You haven't accused the friend of anything— you've simply stated your feelings. If he cares about how you feel and has never thought about the situation, he will probably feel embarrassed, apologize, and offer to remedy the unfairness. If he gets angry and thinks you have no right to complain, do you still want him for a friend?

BETRAYAL

Betrayal by a close friend is much harder to take than slights from casual friends because a person can hurt us in direct proportion to how important he or she is to us. Husbands and wives who divorce often know the pain of betrayal more than those in any other relationship. Still, many teens have felt betrayal from once good friends.

> • My best friend stole my boyfriend. I was so upset and confused that she would choose him over my friendship.
> • I told a friend a very deep secret about myself and later she told one of her other friends and I found out. I felt like I'd been slapped in the face.

When the betrayal is slight—a friend forgets your birthday or smiles when someone else tells a joke at your expense—then possibly re-evaluating your expectations of the friendship is in order. Have you confused a casual friend for a close friend? If so, you can adjust your thinking accordingly and continue the relationship.

But when a close friend's betrayal cuts deeply, only you know how much you can forgive.

HOW TO MAKE REPAIRS

Like flat tires, some friendships will take a new inner tube and roll like new. Others, no matter how many patches you put on the outside, keep going flat. When one of your friendships springs a leak, only you can decide if the friendship is worth the time and emotional energy to repair.

If you do decide to try to clear the air with a friend, remember that you are paying him or her a compliment. If you didn't care about the friendship, you'd simply end it without explanation. Here are some guidelines for talking out problems to arrive at effective solutions:

1. Begin with an honest appreciation of the friendship. For instance, just because your friend has become too possessive doesn't mean that you haven't enjoyed the time you've spent with that friend. Tell him or her how much the friendship has meant to you in the past and how much it means to you now. Remind the friend that that's why you're having the talk.

2. Discuss the problem by sending "I" messages rather than "you" messages. Don't put your friend on the defensive by immediately launching into what he/she has done to you. Rather, state how *you* feel about the situation: "I feel really disappointed when we've planned to go to a movie together and you call at the last minute to say that your boyfriend wants to take you somewhere." (Not, "*You* disappoint me when *you* don't carry through on our plans.") Or say, "I get depressed when you talk so much about your mother's drinking. I worry about you and think about what I can do to help—even late at night when I wake up. I just can't handle it and it's getting me down." (Not, "*You* keep telling me about your mother's drinking and *you* depress me. *You've* got to give me more space.") Try, "I feel like I'm having to pay more than my share for gasoline on the weekends." (Not, "*You're* not being fair to me when *you* always expect me to drive *you* places and never offer to buy gas.")

And don't be afraid to admit your own weaknesses and failures while discussing the problem: "I guess maybe I bring up the debate tournament too much. No wonder you feel like I'm bragging." Or, "I shouldn't have been so gossipy in the first place, and then I wouldn't feel so bad that Yolanda knows what I said."

3. Ask questions about how your friend sees the problem. Often the friend agrees about the rough spots in the relationship and is also ready to correct the problem. On other occasions the friend may be able to tell you what he thinks you are contributing to the situation. Questions like "Don't you think we would be less irritable with each other if we spent more time with other friends, too?" lets the other person save face—as if he is part of the solution rather than the problem.

4. Offer solutions rather than just criticisms. Rather than saying, "I think you impose on me to drive you to work too often," try "I think we should take turns driving to work." Rather than saying, "Every time Marianne is over here and you're around, I feel like you're flirting and I get jealous," try, "What do you say that when I take Marianne out, we don't try to double-date that night."

5. *When you're at fault, apologize sincerely.* When someone says, "Well, I'm sorry," in a huffy voice and stalks away, you definitely know you can file that apology in the wastebasket. People have other subtle ways of apologizing that are really no apology at all. "*If* I've hurt you, I'm sorry" really means "I don't think you should feel hurt over what I did, but if you are, I'll be a big person about it and apologize." You can't blame a friend who senses the insincerity and balks at this kind of apology.

On the other hand, note the difference in this apology: "I did say you had no business trying out for drill team. I was wrong and it was a thoughtless comment. Will you forgive me?" Such a statement shows sincere regret, and most often when you are willing to admit wrongdoing, the other person will be as broadminded and admit his fault too.

6. *Forgive and forget.* "I told a friend something that I never wanted to get further than her. Since she had never betrayed me before, it was a shock to find she had told four other people. I forgave her and think she's a good friend, but I know I can't ever trust her, which hurts," explains Julie.

That's not the kind of forgiveness that will cement a relationship back together. As long as you keep dredging the memory of the betrayal up, it will color your future relationship and limit its growth. True forgiveness means holding no grudge.

HOW TO SAY GOOD-BYES

Sometimes when the hurt has been too deep or when talking it out doesn't help, you will find that you must end a friendship. Often the type of problem indicates how you best can end the relationship. For instance, if you feel that your friend criticizes you too much and damages your self-esteem, you might try to lower the intensity of the friendship by spending less time together. This also might be the answer if your friend manipulates you into doing things that go against your values.

Another way to wind down the friendship is to help the person find another friend or solution to his problem. If you need to get away from a friend who continuously dumps problems on you that you can't handle or blames you for unsatisfactory advice, try to steer her to another solution. Perhaps you could suggest the school counselor or a favorite teacher. Or suggest another person you know who has handled a similar problem well and could offer sympathy and solutions. If a friend gets too possessive, perhaps you could introduce him to other potential friends to occupy his time.

Finally, if these two ways—limiting time you

spend together and helping him find other solutions—fail, you may have to confront your friend head on and tell him or her you no longer want to be friends. This is what happened to Belinda: "My friend and I had been very close for about one year, and one day she said to me that she just didn't feel like being my friend anymore and walked off. I felt terribly upset and sad, and then I was angry that she hadn't said anything about the subject sooner."

A direct confrontation like the one Belinda describes is always difficult, particularly if you haven't prepared the friend ahead of time by trying to discuss the problem. If the friend wants to discuss your reasons for ending the relationship, you owe him or her that courtesy. When such a confrontation turns into an argument, both people feel vulnerable.

Try to make the confrontation as positive as possible. Tell the person that you have benefited from the relationship in the past and that you are a better person because of the friendship but that now the differences between you seem insurmountable. Wish him or her the best in something of current interest (an upcoming tennis season or a new relationship) and then walk away smiling.

Competition, jealousy, possessiveness, criticisms, conflicting values, and betrayal can kill your spirit. When talking over the problem fails to cure the ache, withdrawal may be the only answer.

Ending a friendship takes courage, but whoever said growing up sound and healthy was easy?

Part Two

How to be a Friend to Yourself

Chapter Six

LIKE YOURSELF—WHO ME?

FRIDAY MORNING TOM Layard felt like he might fly right on through his junior year without ever touching down. After the second period announcement that he had been elected class president, his classmates cheered, clapped him on the back, and shouted "speech" until he stood up. He made a mock, low sweeping bow, and announced that his first official duty would be to give sophomores the day off from school.

By noon, he'd been congratulated by half the student body and all his teachers. After school he had two girls he'd dated off and on stop to talk to him in the hall and hint that they were available for the upcoming weekend.

Even the opposing football team that night cooperated with his mood. He completed seven passes and gained over sixty yards rushing.

On Saturday, however, Tom staggered into the

kitchen at eleven to have waffles with his mother and older brother, Mark, home from college for the weekend. After breakfast Mrs. Layard asked Tom to mow the lawn while she and Mark shopped for a new suit he needed for being best man in a friend's upcoming wedding. Grudgingly, Tom pulled out the lawn mower as he watched them drive off toward the mall. Mark cast a big shadow; Tom feared he would always be "little brother."

On Sunday afternoon, Tom called up his best friend Robert to see a movie and stop for pizza. Robert suggested that Tom tell his mother how he felt about doing all the extras around the house while the spending money went to Mark. Robert advised that a part-time job sounded like a good solution.

But later that night in bed, Tom dreaded going to school the next Monday morning. What new ideas did he have for raising money for his class? What if the officers didn't cooperate with him? What if his best friend Robert really knew him— oh, Robert knew he wasn't the clown he came on as in school, but then he certainly didn't know Tom had been scared spitless about the election. And what kind of ingrate was he anyway, when his parents gave him all the spending money he could possibly need? At least Mark didn't know what a jealous, insecure kid brother he had. Or did he? Hours later, Tom willed himself to sleep.

Is this "The Three Lives of Tom"? Not exactly,

but almost. Tom, just like all of us, plays various roles and has more than one self—the public self, the private self, the personal self. At school, he is the self-assured leader, class wit, sought-after date, good student, talented athlete. He is BIG. At home he plays the private role with his family and close friends. He is Mark's little brother with a lot to learn. He is a son distracted with the idea of a part-time job. He's a friend to hang around with when no one feels like impressing anybody else. Finally alone, his personal self takes over. He doubts his leadership abilities as well as his friend's understanding of him. In fact, he decides he's a jealous, insecure kid who doesn't deserve the good fortune he's had.

Which is the real Tom?

All three.

WHO ARE YOU?

Finding out who you are is an extremely difficult adventure. And parents often complicate the task:

> "You're too old to argue with your little sister about a piece of cake. She's five years old. You're grown."
> "Who do you think you are, staying out until 3 a.m.?"
> "Surely you can drive Billie to piano lessons for me once a week."
> "You can't just take the car without telling me where you're going."
> "You're going to clean the garage today;

you're old enough to take on a little responsibility around here and earn your
own money."

"No, you're not old enough to get a part-time
job; all you need to concentrate on is your
English grade."

Who is the real you? Your self-concept involves
your *personality traits* (impulsive, quiet, generous), *abilities* (writing skills, dancing, memory),
attitudes (religious, moral, political), *habits and
actions* (cheerleading, work in library on Saturday,
ride bus to school), and your *likes* and *dislikes*
(chocolate pie, blue, mysteries).

Some people develop their self-concept from
looking in the mirror. But appearance rarely de-
fines. All fat people aren't jolly and all those with
beautifully white, straight teeth won't become
movie stars.

Other teens get their self-image from parents.
Respondents on the survey had this to say about
how their parents contributed to their self-
concept:

- My parents are honest, kind, straightforward, happy people. That's why I hope-
  fully am honest, kind, and straightforward.
- They suggest things I'm good at and
  suggest working on things that need improvement.
- They always tell me how neat I am.
- They have taught me to earn my keep.
  They have taught me to respect others'
  property and feelings.

- They help me to be responsible and mature.

But not all contributions from parents are positive:

- They have protected me too much.
- My mother makes me self-conscious because I know she likes my sister better than me.
- I love my dad, but he has made me so scared. I'm really paranoid at times.
- They've really lowered my confidence and messed up my life.

Although these teens are aware of either positive and negative vibes from their parents, some are unaware of the subtle ways their parents make them feel mature, responsible, dependable, scared, or overprotected. Ideas about ourselves slip into our consciousness slowly—incident by incident, comment by comment. When Ken handled his little brother's bleeding chin and got him to the emergency room for stitches, he was labeled mature. When Lori called home to tell her dad she'd had car trouble and would be late, her dad commented that she was dependable. In the second grade, when Bryan told his mother about a bully who shoved him around on the bus, she got uptight and started meeting him at the bus stop. Bryan learned to believe that he couldn't handle the situation alone, that he needed someone bigger to protect him.

Feedback from parents about *who* we are and

how we are also comes in nonverbal ways. Perhaps your parent says he loves you, but never spends time with you, never hugs and kisses you, never looks you directly in the eye. You may feel that you are no fun to be with, that you have nothing interesting to say, that you are unlovable, or that you are unimportant.

Finally, your position in the family (older, younger, middle, only child) influences your self-concept. As the oldest, you may learn that you always should get more privileges and spending money than others. As the youngest, you may learn that losing your temper or crying or pouting makes everyone else give in to your wishes.

In addition to appearance and parental feedback, teachers and school influence your self-concept. Respondents on the survey had this to say about the way teachers and school affected them both positively and negatively:

- Since I am a good student, teachers have praised me and recommended me for certain honors. This makes me feel good about myself.
- They have lowered my self-image because I don't do well in school.
- Because I'm active in school activities, I'm treated like I'm important.
- My coaches make me feel like I really accomplish something.
- They show me there are more people,

places, and events than my parents know or care about.
- They have helped me learn that everything does not always go my way.
- They helped me see that I can handle everyday things.
- My school makes it hard for you to be positive because people are very critical.
- I've come to expect at least a B and expect nothing else from myself.

How do teachers and classmates instill or reinforce these self-images in teens? Again, through a variety of ways. Tone of voice and eye contact from other people provide clues to whom they think we are. Educational psychologists say teachers give "warm time" to students they like and "cool time" to students they dislike.

Other feedback from teachers and school is more tangible—IQ tests and ability grouping. But again, this feedback on the real you is misleading. IQ test scores do not remain constant. Scores are only guides and you shouldn't let them label your academic abilities. Often kids get placed in a "slow" group, come to think of themselves as incapable, and fail to work up to their true potential. Other kids get placed in a "high" group, make Cs for the year and feel like failures, not realizing that they were performing above most of their peers in the "average" group.

Classmates, as well as teachers, can give you either correct or incorrect feedback about how you are. If you like to read a lot, they may assume you are superintelligent and make good grades. But teachers' and classmates' input into your self-concept is not always unsolicited. Many teens try comparing themselves to others to decide if they are above, equal to, or below everyone else. When asked how she compared socially with her peers, one sixteen-year-old said: "I excel in most all areas—intelligence, wit good looks. But then I'm the only one I know as well as me." However, another teen confided: "I really don't feel equal to others. I'm not too smart, not interesting, and definitely not good-looking." A third teen has the right idea: "I don't judge people's looks or intelligence to compare myself with them. Individuality is important."

After assembling on the mind's computer the data from parents, family, teachers, and peers, you may find it difficult to decide how accurate opinions of you really are. Some teens say the composite picture truly reflects who they are. Others say the images are contradictory:

- Most people see me as a leader and they feel I go after things I want. But I really personally think I'm not that much of a leader. I have a number of flaws I could improve and have a lot to learn.
- My school group sees me as shy, dull, intelligent. My skating group sees me as wild, hyper, quick, capricious, mysterious and a free spirit.
- My parents see me as a goody-two-shoes, and I'm not.
- I'm really nice and understanding and

others think I'm a snob and smart mouth.
- Some people see me as an airhead, but I'm really pretty smart.
- On the inside, I'm really a clean-cut boy, but on the outside I'm a druggie. I want to quit but I like my friends, too.
- Some people see me as someone who is wasting my life away, but I feel I am working toward a goal I have set for myself.
- They see me as an ugly football player. I feel that I'm a nice, gentle, loving person.

HOW TO SHED LIMITING LABELS

No matter if you've been labeled a "blue-ribbon winner" or "last place," only you can find the real you. You have to decide for yourself if you are fat like your brother says or beautiful like your dad says. Remember that although labels are convenient, they are often based on little concrete information and often come from someone else's personal prejudice or perception.

When you are younger, you act very nearly as expected and labeled. In other words, you see yourself as your parents, teachers, and friends see you. But as you get older, you can begin to reshuffle the data and come up with a more accurate picture.

To get an accurate reading, don't compare yourself to the "best." Terri, 15, says: "I feel so dumb compared with two of my friends who make all As." But why should she compare herself with those two. Why not compare herself to the majority who make Cs? Why compare your pitching skills to Nolan Ryan's or your figure to Brooke Shield's? Give yourself a break by making fair comparisons.

The problem with flaws is that we don't confine them to a small pocket of our life. We reason: "I made an F in math, so I must be stupid. If I'm stupid, probably nothing I say makes sense to other people. Since probably nothing I say makes sense to people, I should keep my mouth shut. Nobody likes shy, quiet people, so nobody likes me." You can see the danger to self-concept of this avalanche of faulty reasoning.

And feeling negative about yourself gives off bad vibes to those around you, which make people want to get away from you to protect themselves. Thus, the downward cycle continues.

It's up to you to shed negative feedback and to assemble an accurate image. Nothing is so important to your good mental health as the estimate you place on yourself. I remember the college professor who taught my creative writing class. It was nothing she actually said, but rather an amused smile and patronizing tone that discouraged my first attempts at writing. When the final grade came—a B instead of the A I expected—I thought seriously of giving up my dream. She'd taught writing at that university for almost twenty-five years. She should know poor writing when she sees it, right? That's how I felt for almost two weeks, and then on a whim I sent off an article to a magazine editor and made a sale.

Shortly thereafter, I sold a book and then another and another. But I've never completely forgotten that teacher's first negative feedback. When each successive book comes out, I'm tempted to mail her a copy with a note saying, "So there!"

ASSESSING YOUR STRENGTHS AND WEAKNESSES

In a nationwide 1980 survey of more than 160,000 teens, researchers Jane Norman and Myron Harris found that seven out of ten teens like themselves when all is said and done. That does not mean that they have put on blinders to all the negatives, but rather that after tallying the good and bad points, they have decided the good outweighs the bad.

One evening in the car with my five-year-old daughter, she commented that Nancy (a friend of hers) always came in last when she ran foot races at school, but that she colored better than anyone in the whole class. She added, "Everyone has things they do good and things they do bad. Like I'm good in numbers, reading, and turning flips, and I'm not good in. . ." She paused pensively, then concluded, "I can't think of anything I'm not good in."

I only smiled, offering no contradiction. Someone would burst her bubble soon enough.

As a teen, you know better. In my survey of 215 students, eight percent said they liked everything about themselves; six percent said they liked nothing about themselves. Both assessments are blinding and limiting. But some people never get around to making a true assessment of their strengths and weaknesses.

Some teens stop their personal growth by using various defense mechanisms rather than admitting weaknesses. Some deny failure: "I could have passed that test, but I didn't really try." Some rationalize: "I didn't make the team, but then football is a waste of time anyway." Some project the weakness on to other people or events or circumstances: "The coaches are all nearsighted."

Other teens stop before they reach their potential by covering up their strengths: "My painting won, but it was sheer luck."

If you're having trouble getting a fair picture of yourself, take a few minutes to assemble some new data. Make a list of good things about yourself—your habits, skills, appearance, personality traits. Think of compliments others have paid you, rewards and contests you've won. To get you started, here is a partial list of things teens in the survey said they liked about themselves:

patient	dependable	loyal
athletic	helpful	nice smile
accepting of	confident	common sense
others	honest	rational
talented dancer	always do my	sense of humor
open	best	tolerant
creative	involved	

objective understanding height
determined easygoing hard worker
organized courteous independent
good listener good morals intelligent
stick by my aggressive friendly
  convictions hair nice
self-disciplined

Now, on another paper list some of your weaknesses. Here are some things the high-schoolers did not like about themselves:

too demanding shy no enthusiasm
not serious jealous cold
  enough too sensitive forgetful
don't try moody sarcastic
smart mouth lazy spoiled
critical smoking short temper
feel insecure weight gossip
hair teeth inconsiderate
impatient scars exaggerate
too emotional eyes no goals
indecisive stubborn freckles
snobbish tactless eyebrows
secretive

Did you have a problem deciding on which list to put some of your traits? Some are both good and bad, if taken to the extreme. For instance, you might be loyal (strength) to your friends, but vengeful (weakness) to outsiders who don't like your friend. You may be arrogant (weakness) rather than confident (strength). You may be impulsive (strength) when you're out with your friends and thus, do crazy things that they consider fun. On the other hand, you may impulsively (weakness) quit your job because of an upcoming party and later regret the loss of spending money.

These "opposite" traits are what make us real. You may have learned in a creative writing class that when you develop characters for a story, they should have at least one strong trait and one weak or opposite one. For instance, your heroine may have strong ambitions and want to change school policy. But she may also be shy and afraid to run for election to the Student Council. Her shyness thwarts her ambition.

On a third paper, list some of your good-bad traits.

What to do with the lists when you're finished? First, look at the list of good traits and pat yourself on the back. Maybe you're not used to praising yourself, but you should get used to it. You deserve credit. If you make good grades, don't say that the work is easy. If you kick a field goal, don't say nobody could have missed. Not only do you have to accept your good traits intellectually, you have to accept them emotionally. You can't just know you win awards in ice-skating, you have to *feel* that you excel. It's the difference between knowing you're intelligent and actually enrolling in French III. One way to develop more self-confidence about strengths, says Dale Carnegie in his book *How To Win Friends and Influence People,* is to do the things you fear and get a record of successful experiences behind you.

Now to the list of weaknesses and the list of good-bad traits. Mark the ones that you can control or modify. These take a conscious effort to turn into strengths. We'll come back to them and how you can begin to minimize or control them in Chapter 7.

Finally, cross through the weaknesses that are impossible to change. What do you do with those? Accept them. How are you going to accept other people or ask them to accept you if you can't accept your own weaknesses?

When you become preoccupied with these weaknesses, you turn onto a downward course. You begin to compare yourself with others (usually others who are extremely good in this skill or trait) and feel inadequate. Then because you feel inadequate, you fear everyone else will reject you.

To fight off this imagined rejection, you begin to openly criticize yourself, hoping that someone will contradict you and compliment you; you may cover up these feelings of inferiority by acting superior and sophisticated; you may withdraw from people, so they can't reject you; you may exaggerate your attempts to make them like you by being too generous with your money, letting them copy your homework, or showering them with flattery. Of course, such exaggerated attempts to buy acceptance from others usually make people uncomfortable after a while.

Eventually, they reject you—but not for the reason you first imagined. As I said, a poor self-concept is a downward, vicious spiral.

Sifting through the layers of your personality—
the way you behave in school, the way you behave with your family and close friends, the way
you feel, think, and act when you're alone—is a
difficult task. Incorrect data may have filtered into
your self-concept from your parents, teachers,
classmates, and friends. If so, shed negative
labels others may have placed on you and dis-
cover your own self-worth. Be proud of your
strengths.

There is no permanent "you." You are what you
choose to be each day.

Chapter Seven

A CRASH COURSE IN SELF-IMPROVEMENT

How do you react to criticism? What would you say if the teacher returned an English composition on which you'd made the lowest grade in the class? What would you say if your brother told you that your tennis serve in the last match was lousy? How about if your best friend commented that you'd been cynical and grouchy lately?

If you're like the majority, criticism is hard to take straight on. Most people react in one of four ways:

1. They become defensive. To the teacher: "I didn't have time to do the paper well because we had a swim meet over the weekend." To the brother: "My serve was lousy because of the puddles on the court." To the best friend: "I have plenty to be grouchy about; Dad has been on my case all weekend."

2. *They attack.* They focus the spotlight away from themselves onto someone else who is at fault. To the teacher: "I did lousy on the composition because you didn't give clear directions about what you wanted." To the brother: "If you think the serve was so bad, I'd like to see you do better. You didn't even make the team." To the best friend: "Well, you haven't been Miss Cheery yourself. I'm tired of hearing you complain about doing that stupid science project."

3. *They withdraw, feeling guilty and inadequate.* If they get a bad grade, they ask no questions about the mark, but rather tuck the paper into their notebooks and decide there's no use trying anymore. If a brother criticizes the tennis serve, they say he's right, that they should never have tried out for the team anyway, and they quit. If a best friend says they're grouchy, they decide the friend doesn't like them anymore, so they stop calling or inviting him to go any place.

4. *They consider the criticism and evaluate it for themselves to see if it's valid.* If it isn't an accurate assessment, they discard it with their self-esteem intact. If the criticism points out a needed change, they try to make the improvement. They ask the teacher to explain the mistakes they don't understand and ask for help for the next paper. They ask the brother if he could see from the stands what they were doing differently that affected the serve. If the friend was correct about the cynical, grouchy disposition,

they try to figure out how to settle the dispute with Dad.

If you typically react to criticism by defending yourself, by attacking others, or by withdrawing, then you're probably experiencing a lot of emotional pain without much healing. When you fail to use criticism to your advantage, you suffer the pain of the critical remark without hope for a cure.

That's what this chapter is all about—using criticism to its best end. Chapter 6 mentions that having a healthy self-concept involves assessing your strengths and weaknesses. You should pat yourself on the back for your strengths, then divide the weaknesses into two piles. The things you can't change (your height, the financial status of your parents), you accept. The weaknesses that can be changed (a smoking habit, an irritable disposition, disloyalty), you work on.

The remainder of the chapter will help you do just that.

SHYNESS

Eighty percent of the American population, researcher and writer Philip Zimbardo has discovered, have considered themselves shy sometime during their lives: Forty percent say they are presently shy. And most of these think of shyness as a weakness that limits their freedom and enjoyment in life. The teens in my survey agreed:

- I hate it when I have to give oral reports in front of class. I'm certainly more shy than anybody else. I wish I fit in.
- People see me as a very shy, quiet person. Actually, I love to act crazy and have fun and laugh and be active. Fortunately, I do have a few close friends I can be myself with.
- I think only two people (my best friend and my ex-boyfriend) have seen the true me, because when I go out and meet people and at school, I'm real outgoing and hyper. But the true me is a homebody and very shy and very quiet.
- People see me as a shy, smart individual with a good future figured out. I see myself as a shy average individual who is scared stiff about my future.

Even Miss Americas are shy. Donna Axum, Miss America, 1964, writes: "When I was a child of ten or eleven, I was very shy and tense about meeting people as I was extremely self-conscious of my gangly appearance." TV talk show hosts, politicians, and athletes join her in claiming shyness.

Although most people don't consider shyness in others a great weakness, the shy dislike the trait in themselves. Of course, for those who want to defend their shyness and/or blame others, they can have a field day. Difficulties in school, unfavorable comparisons with older kids in the family, moving and changing schools and lifestyles, or having shy parents as role models can cause shyness. But defending yourself and blaming others will limit your freedom all your life.

If you want to overcome shyness, you can. We have shy women on the Miss America walkway and shy athletes giving locker room interviews for an audience of millions. According to Zimbardo, forty percent of those who were once shy say that they have overcome their shyness—although it took hard work.

Over fifty percent of those in my high school survey who said they tried to overcome shyness did so by *forcing* themselves to talk to other people. If talking to classmates or people you know seems too risky, practice conversations with strangers. Talk to the kid in the dentist's office for a brace adjustment. Talk to the salesclerk about what pant styles seem to be selling best. Call a radio station and ask how they select records to play and turn in a request. Ask somebody for directions. Gradually, you'll feel more comfortable and will be able to strike up a meaningful conversation with anyone.

Other suggestions from teens: 1) Study the situation and try to act like the others around you. 2) Get used to new surroundings beforehand. 3) Laugh and smile at what other people say. 4) Think positive and take deep breaths to relax.

Essentially, the shy person has to accept responsibility for himself. Although most teens say they try to help a shy person become part of the group, their efforts are limited.

• I ignore shy people. I don't make fun of

them though because I myself used to be shy. But I don't want to get involved.

- Sometimes I will talk to them and try to make them feel wanted. Most of the time I just ignore them because I don't want to take time out to be nice. Isn't that awful? I know that's not the thing to do, but I just can't help it.

- I try to break the ice, but if that doesn't work, I'd leave them alone. I'd figure they didn't want to be bothered.

- I just ignore them because I mean it's his problem, not mine. If he's going to be shy all the time, he won't get very far in life. The sooner he snaps out of it, the better.

- I try to talk to the person, but it makes me nervous to talk to a nervous person. I run out of things to say. If they stay in their shell forever, I will eventually forget them.

- I used to be shy, but now I'm more confident in myself. I usually try to talk to them just about something small to make them feel wanted. I will admit that it is hard, but at least I try, and I can't say that for most people of my age group.

Again, I repeat, the majority of teens said they would try to help the shy person into the group, but after an initial, brief effort, the shy person must take the initiative and reach out.

Some people actually like being shy. Shyness can guarantee you more personal freedom in that you don't have to be involved with people you don't like. You can stand back and analyze before approving others. And shy people rarely are considered bossy or braggarts. You also get called on less to do things that you might not want to do.

But consider the difference between a passive, shy person and one who is either assertive or aggressive. An overly aggressive person barges into conversations, brags, does crazy things to draw attention to himself. He hurts people's feelings and gets his way regardless. His tone is loud and snappy and demanding. His whole body seems to direct the situation and manipulate people.

The other extreme, a passive, shy person, stands back during conversations and rarely expresses an opinion. He apologizes when somebody disagrees with him. He takes insults without making a response. He speaks in low, apologetic tones and looks at the floor or away from the people he is talking to.

Between these two extremes is the assertive person. He considers himself equal in conversations with others; he listens to others' opinions and gives his own. His voice sounds natural and relaxed, and he looks at others while he talks to them. He doesn't run over people, and he doesn't allow them to run over him.

Passivity is self-destructive and aggression elicits hostility in others. But an assertive person builds self-esteem while commanding respect from others—goals worth striving for.

HUMOR

"I walked through the cafeteria and this group of kids was standing in a circle around this pile of lunch trays in the middle of the floor. Nobody was saying anything, just staring. It was really funny," said Michael.

"Do you mean funny 'ha-ha' or funny 'strange'?" Leon asked.

Just as there are two meanings for funny, humor, too, means different things to different people. Humor can mean cracking jokes, but it also means looking at life in an amused way. Some humor can be cute and kind—other humor is hostile and hurtful.

When Bradley makes a wisecrack about Nan in class, everybody breaks up—including Nan. Because he means no harm, everyone feels free to laugh. On the other hand, in the same class Brenda makes a crack about Nan and only a few smile. Nan blushes and is offended. The classroom gets tense. What's the difference? The subject of the humor and the way it was done.

Teasing people about things they may be sensitive about—appearance, skills, handicaps—with the intent to embarrass is rarely humorous to onlookers.

To develop a positive sense of humor, learn first of all to laugh at yourself. If you're a lousy baseball player, you'll be found out sooner or later, so you may as well make a crack about your .007 batting average and not take the game so seriously. When you laugh at your own mistakes, others laugh with you—not at you.

Second, learn to see the humor in troublesome situations. This is the kind of attitude that makes someone, while watching a wrecker pull his car from the ditch to the mechanic shop, remark, "I bet this beats the gas mileage I've been getting."

A positive sense of humor attracts people; a hostile humor repels them.

OBNOXIOUS BEHAVIOR

What do you consider obnoxious behavior from your peers? What attitudes, activities, characteristics, or behavior would cause you not to want to become friends with someone?

I asked this question of the 215 high schoolers. The remainder of the chapter includes their answers. Skim the headings, and if you think any of the particular subjects may be a problem in your own personality, consider the suggestions for improvements.

ADDICT.

Thirty percent of the teens mentioned either smoking, drinking, drugs or all three as habits they found undesirable in a friend.

> • I don't like people who drink so much they lose touch with reality or who are on drugs and have negative attitudes like this and can't control themselves.
> • I think drinking, smoking, or saying disgusting things is obnoxious. I like to drink

with dinner but not get drunk in public on a Friday or Saturday night. So I probably wouldn't be friends with someone who did these things.

• I'm a person who doesn't drink, smoke, or have sex in high school. One of the most obnoxious things to me is a drunk person or one who brags about what he did while he was drunk on Friday night.

Others mentioned "side-effects" of these habits—the smell of smoke, offensive language while drunk, or having someone vomit on their possessions due to drunkenness.

Perhaps the days of taking up one of these habits "to be accepted" with peers is gone. Perhaps surprising to many, the survey showed that one in three teens would cross you off their list of friends for these habits alone.

If you have problems with one of these addictions, talk to your school counselor in getting help to overcome it. The life you're damaging is your own.

BEING A LOUDMOUTH.

Some people cover up their uneasiness by being a clown. Others create the same commotion around themselves to get attention. For many, it's the wrong kind of attention.

• I don't like people if they talk back to a teacher with smart remarks or if they're real loud at a football game or pep rally. I mean

loud, saying things that don't pertain to the
cheers.
• Obnoxious person? One that's seventeen
and still jumps up and down screaming and
running down the halls.
• I consider obnoxious behavior from peers
as always trying to be the center of attention. Talking excessively, especially when
saying nothing—constantly repeating
themselves.
• When they're loud and boisterous and always making a disturbance.
• I can't stand loudmouthed, showoff guys or
girls who flirt and act really stupid in front
of guys.

If you see yourself in some of these statements,
perhaps being aware of your loudness will help
you tone it down when out in public. If you're
trying to cover uneasiness, work on building your
self-esteem in the area of your weakness,
eliminating the need to "cover" by distractions.
While negative attention may be better than no
attention at all, positive attention is a more re-
warding goal.

SNOB.

Why do people act snobbish? Some teens, who
can't express negative feelings to their parents or
other authorities, take out their frustrations on
those they consider weaker than they are. Other
teens have been taught by parents to look down
on "inferiors"—those who "only" make Bs,

those of another race, those who live in another neighborhood.

Still others act snobbish as a defense. Teens who say classmates of the same age bore them probably are covering up for a fear that their peers will not accept them. In other words, their philosophy is to reject others before others reject them.

The language of snobbery can be subtle. Someone complains about not having enough time to swim in his backyard pool. Some kids flaunt money—others, popularity or grades. Some who behave like snobs, though they may not brag, remain indifferent and aloof to those around them. Peers react strongly to this behavior:

- I hate the "think they're God when they're not" type people.
- People who are stuck-up and talk about spending a fortune in clothes and jewelry really bother me.
- What I dislike the most is when a person suddenly starts acting older than he or she really is. They don't realize what they're missing by acting so mature. Usually, they come across as really stuck-up people.
- I hate it when people think they are better than others. If someone was supernice to me but mean to someone else, I still would not be friends with them.
- I hate it when people are conceited and try to act popular, bragging about themselves. Our next-door neighbor brags about her daughter to us all of the time. Now we love her and her mother, but it just gets to

be too much. Her daughter gets As on everything. She hasn't made a B since fifth grade. We know she's smart, but they rub it in.
• I hate being around people who make me feel like less.

If you have picked up some of the language and action of snobbishness, reconsider. All people have some valuable insights and skills. It's to your advantage not to cut yourself off from what others offer to enrich your life. Rather than raising you on the social scale, snobbery lowers you on the popularity poll.

RIDICULER.

In any society there will always be those scavengers who feed on others' misfortunes. They ridicule people with a disability, those who live in a poorer section of town, or those who weigh too much. Going one step further than the snob who ignores his "inferiors," the ridiculer flagrantly hurts others. And by hurting others, he hopes to bolster his own sagging self-esteem.

Still other ridiculers cut down those whom they consider their superiors. Because they can't make good grades, they make fun of those who do. If they can't get a boyfriend or girlfriend, they belittle another teen who can.

Whether you cut down someone "above" or "below" you, you actually lower yourself in the eyes of those who observe this behavior:

- I hate those who are rude to others or make fun of people who are handicapped.
- I can't stand it when a person puts someone else down. Especially when they keep doing it in front of an entire class. I wouldn't want to be friends with someone who never had anything nice or good to say about other people or things.
- I really hate it when people ridicule and cut down people because of their looks, race—something they can't help. They drive me up the wall.
- I hate when they cut people down, try to act cool in front of people by making someone else look bad.

If you catch yourself ridiculing others, examine your motives. Do you feel threatened by them in some way? If so, work on the flaw in your personality rather than trying to mask it by hurting someone else. You never raise yourself by lowering someone else.

POOR ME.

A teenage department store clerk walked over to me after a particularly rough Saturday morning with customers and asked: "Do I have a sign across my forehead that says 'Gripe Here'?"

Although I laughed and assured her that she did not, I do frequently run into people who wear "Kick Me" signs. Not paper signs, but ones no less striking and visible—body language. This "Kick Me" signbearer walks stooped, avoids eye contact, speaks in a mumble, and nervously fidgets.

In addition to the body language, the person with the poor-me attitude constantly puts himself down, a particularly irritating habit to people who compliment him.

Feeling uncomfortable when receiving a compliment seems to be common among teens:

> • I think a compliment is hard. When I'm given a compliment I always feel they're being sarcastic.
> • I find it hard to believe that someone should think I'm pretty and not fat. My friends always say I never give myself a break.
> • I find getting compliments difficult because I don't agree. I'm not a good person, so why compliment me?
> • I guess I have always been cut down, so now when I get compliments, it's hard to believe.

Generally, people refuse compliments because they feel badly about themselves. Others refuse compliments because they simply don't know what to say.

Some teens have the notion that accepting a compliment is being conceited. Dave admits: "No, it doesn't bother me when people compliment me, but I try to act like it does." He's got the wrong idea. Accepting praise doesn't mean snobbery. It's an act of appreciation.

"If you receive a compliment, like someone

says your hair looks good, and you say 'no, it doesn't,' it makes the other person feel stupid," Jodie explains. To compliment someone and have him or her dispute your compliment is much like smiling at someone and having them slap a pie in your face.

So what to say? A simple "thank you" is enough. Or, you can add another comment stating your feelings about the situation. Let me illustrate:

Compliment:
> "I like that dress."

Poor me:
> "I wore it last year. It's old." (You've told the person that he or she is unobservant and has bad taste.)

Better:
> "Thank you. My older sister let me borrow it. I'll tell her you think she has good taste."

Compliment:
> "You pitched a good game yesterday."

Poor me:
> "You're full of bull. We got our teeth kicked in." (You've attacked the person.)

Better:
> "Thanks. I wasn't sure I could hang in the last inning, though. They had some good batters."

Compliment:
> "You always make good grades."

Poor me:

"No, I don't." (You've contradicted the person—called him or her a liar.)

Better:

"Thanks for the vote of confidence. I try to keep telling myself that every time I get worried on a test."

Compliment:

"You got a haircut. I like it."

Poor me:

"She cut it too short. It looks ridiculous." (He doesn't know what he's talking about or he's lying to you.)

Better:

"Thanks. I think it's a little too short, but it'll grow."

Inappropriate responses make the complimenter feel foolish, wrong, or attacked. When you catch yourself refusing praise, stop in midsentence, smile, and take what has been offered in the spirit it was given.

Finally, in the same vein as refusing compliments is the habit of running yourself down in the hopes that someone will contradict you. When you say: "I always look fat. Why can't I be like you and look good in my clothes?" you are fishing for a contradiction and most people find this habit irritating. When compliments are given sincerely, appreciate them. But don't fish.

APPLE-POLISHER.

"Snowing" or "doing a number"—whatever the current term in your school, you probably know kids who try to manipulate people by flattering them. The big difference between flattery and compliments is sincerity. One teen admits: "I never believe nice things people say to me, because I often say things that I don't mean and I figure that's what other people do too."

Comments like, "You're good enough to be on a pro team already," or "You've got to be the smartest student we've ever had at this school," ring with insincerity. Most people recognize insincerity when they hear it.

When you flatter someone and get a blank stare or reserved response, you know that the person sees through the flattery.

GOSSIP.

Some people can't resist the temptation to tell a good story for a laugh at another's expense. Others join a gossipy conversation and agree with what's being said to get "in" with the "right" crowd.

If others gossip to you about someone else, you can be sure they gossip to others about you. It's a deadly game all around. Remember that you can never be a nonparticipant when you hear juicy tidbits about someone. Unless you stop it, you encourage it.

To stop gossip that you didn't originate, you can do one of several things. First, you can state your own position in a nice, but firm way. If someone tells you that Jana usually stays drunk all weekend, you can say that you're not sure you believe that because you've seen her several times on the weekend when she was perfectly sober. You haven't put the gossiper down, but neither have you accepted his or her word without doubt.

Second, you can change the subject. If you don't know anything about what Jana does on the weekend, you can change directions with, "By the way, what did you do last weekend? Or, you might relate what you did. The gossiper will get the hint without your having to hit him or her over the head.

Third, Barbara Walters suggests responding to gossip with the classic line that goes something like this: "That's strange you should say that. Jana always seems to speak so well of you."

If you find *yourself* the subject of gossip, direct confrontation rather than retaliation is a good idea. Perhaps the person whom you think has started the rumor really said something quite different. You can clear up such misunderstandings by saying something like, "I heard that you said I was just dating Charles because he played football. I wanted to check with you to see if you really said that or what you meant exactly." If there was a misunderstanding, you can clear it up immediately. If the gossip was malicious, you have most likely stopped it by letting the person know you are capable of defending yourself.

If you are the gossiper, sooner or later you will realize that your friendships are short-lived. By gossiping to someone, you advertise that you have a bad habit and the Jana in your life will come to realize—if she hasn't already—that if you gossip to her about Cheryl, then you'll gossip to Cheryl about her.

If you're serious about breaking this habit, you can ask your best friend to help by reminding you when you start to cut other people down. Also, you might consider a reward system for yourself. At the end of the day, if you haven't said anything bad about anybody, treat yourself to a movie or a nice verbal pat on the back.

PRANKSTER.

"Bug and thou shalt be bugged in return," is teacher Jess Lair's law in the classroom. Perhaps you've meant no harm by mischievous pranks like plugging bathroom sinks with paper so that they overflow, unscrewing tops to the salt and pepper shakers in the Pizza Palace, or pouring ink all over someone's notebook. But what's fun for the prankster is often pain for the recipient.

> • What really bugs me is a senior in high school acting really silly. I've been with some guys who acted normal in school but at activities, I didn't want to be seen with them. Girls would not have even taken a

> second look and parents think they're not even in junior high.
> • Obnoxious behavior is immature behavior—throwing things, having tantrums, hitting things, breaking and damaging things.

The next time you start to pull a funny, ask yourself if others will think your trick is equally cute. Remember, "Bug and thou shalt be bugged."

GROUCH.

Oscar the Grouch from Sesame Street probably brought a few laughs to you as a child. But if you happened to choose him for a role model, you're probably not winning friends and influencing people. Here's what teens have to say about the Oscars of the world:

> • If someone is rude, corrupt, and always negative about themselves and the world around them, I choose to avoid them and make friends with the people of opposite description.
> • I cannot stand a negative attitude and pessimism! This is very irritating to me.
> • Someone who is always down and never in a good mood depresses me.

The world is so full of gloom and doom reported daily on the TV and in the newspaper that people seek relief from their friends.

If you've been a grouch all your life, possibly you modeled yourself after a parent who eats sour grapes every morning for breakfast. Although highly contagious, irritability is *not* hereditary. You can make a rational decision to overcome a critical, negative outlook.

If mornings seem to cause the most problems, try getting up earlier so you can pull yourself together before facing the world. A fellow classmate of mine, Kurt, used to come in tardy about three mornings out of five. And when he happened to be in class on time and was called on, his response sounded more like a growl than intelligible English. During the first few weeks, his disposition was a joke to the rest of the class. After a few months, everyone avoided him.

If being a grouch is a full-time occupation with you, there's no need to advertise. Grumble to yourself and paste on a smile for onlookers.

SLOB.

Trash mysteriously piles up around a sloppy person's desk. Papers hang out of the locker. The poster you made jointly as part of a class project has egg yolk on it. The car he or she drives looks like floodwaters rushed through the lowered windows. Wrinkled, stained clothes with missing buttons and smelly odors make you wonder if maybe the person dresses in the dark.

The disease elicits sympathy, but friends stay away for fear of contamination.

Good grooming makes an ordinary person attractive and a clean, organized environment spells efficiency.

Have you discovered one or two things you need to do or to avoid doing in order to improve your personality? The encouraging thing is that all the undesirables mentioned can be remedied with work and willpower. You'll feel better about yourself and others will too when you drop bad habits from your repertoire.

Chapter Eight
GETTING OVER DEPRESSION

BEING ALONE IS not a subversive Un-American activity—although were you catapulted from outer space to eavesdrop on our planet you might think so: "He's a real loner, stays to himself," someone whispers in a sinister tone. "She'd rather stay home and read a book," mocks a teenager. "If you don't behave at Grandma's, we're going to leave you at home by yourself next time," a mother scolds. "Use Breathfresh toothpaste and you won't find yourself sitting home alone on Friday nights," advertisers promise.

Despite what we hear to the contrary, aloneness can be beneficial. If you don't believe it, wait until you spend a week's vacation with four family members in a motel room, watching it rain outside. You all become irritable, restless and hyper. People need time to be alone, and many teens find being alone, rather than depressing, a pleasant change of pace:

> • When everyone in the house goes out and I stay home, I enjoy it. I like to be by myself to listen to music or to read.
> • I like to go to a movie alone that gets close to me. It makes me think about what I have and don't have. Being by myself solves my problems.
> • I think of myself as a companion. Living where I do, it's hard to be lonely in school or even in the house.
> • I like to be alone to gather my thoughts.

Enjoying aloneness is an indication of maturity and a good self-concept. Contrary to the stereotype of "lonely old people," researcher Mary Brown Parlee found that as people grow older they feel lonely less often. Seventy-nine percent of the teens under eighteen that she surveyed said they felt lonely "sometimes" or "often." Only thirty-three percent of those over fifty-five felt loneliness to the same degree.

The teen who enjoys solitude draws on his own inner strengths and resources to entertain himself, to get in touch with his real values and goals, to improve himself.

Aloneness becomes negative only when you begin to feel lonely and depressed. For many teens who have not learned to accept themselves and who have not built inner strengths, having friends around is a must. "I feel lonely when I don't have friends with me," Melodie, 16, says. "I

get depressed because I can't stand being alone."
Teens who suffer the compulsion to be constantly
flanked by friends report feeling most lonely
when their activities require separation—
summer, Sundays, late at night, early in the morning.

Both the source and cure for chronic loneliness
and depression lie within yourself. If that's true,
then far from making you more depressed, you
can be optimistic because you can *do* something
about the feeling. When you control your own
feelings, you can steer to a smoother course.

WHAT CAUSES DEPRESSION?

ANGER.

Many teens feel depressed because of bottled up
anger toward other people or circumstances. Parents are a prime target of anger—sometimes they
haven't paid enough attention to you, sometimes
they have destroyed your confidence, sometimes
they deal unfairly with you, sometimes they force
unpleasant circumstances on you.

"I feel really depressed sometimes—like last
Friday night when I went to the football game.
Since I just moved here, I don't know a whole
bunch of people yet. I hate it here and all I could
think of was—'If I was back in my other school,'"
explains Sheryl. Other teens are angry about their
parents' divorce because they feel helpless to
control their own destiny and lifestyle.

Sometimes teens feel angry at circumstances. Barbara complained, "When I broke my wrist and I had to sit out of volleyball, I got really depressed. I just had to keep reminding myself that it [the cast] would soon come off."

Finally, anger often comes from hurt pride. Someone didn't invite you to a party; you didn't make the varsity; a classmate dresses beyond your pocketbook.

When you can't talk or work out your anger, it festers inside and oozes all over your emotional outlook.

GUILT AND WORRY.

When anger is turned inward, we call it guilt. Teens feel guilty over bad grades, eating too much, disappointing parents, not standing up for their rights, bad decisions. Sometimes they even feel bad about feeling bad!

And all the guilt feelings lead to worry about "the next time." Cindi says, "I worry a lot. I lost ten pounds just because of worry—I'm serious. I wish I didn't. I always expect things to turn out for the worst."

Fear of failure or repetition of past mistakes is a vicious circle. Because you're worrying about the last bad test grade, you find it hard to concentrate on the upcoming exam. And sure enough, you fail the second exam, because you couldn't keep your mind on studying. Or, you don't put forth your best effort; so that if you fail, you can shield your pride by saying you failed because you didn't really try.

Some people do the same thing with decisions. They feel guilty over a bad decision. Since they fear another bad decision, they put off making a decision at all. Then when pressured by a deadline, they have to make a hasty decision, which turns out to be wrong. Thus, another bad decision and more guilt and enough worry left over for next time.

Unreal Expectations.

Some teens have never been taught how to handle disappointments. How many times have you seen a small child in a store begging, crying, stomping, and yelling for a new toy? Condemning him as a spoiled brat, we think he probably deserves a good swat.

Yet, frequently the rest of us are guilty of the same unreal expectations. But rather than throwing a fit, we get depressed. Occasionally, we have unreal expectations of ourselves. Susan says: "When I try to do so much, I run out of energy and still have more to do. I feel depressed and sit down and cry for awhile and then get up and go again." It's disappointing to find out that we all have limits to our endurance.

At other times, we expect too much of our parents. Tammy says: "I usually am depressed because I don't have half of the things I really want.

I try to be thankful for what I do have. But there's so much more . . ."

Just as parents sometimes expect too much of their kids (older sister Mary whizzed through math, why can't you?), teens sometimes expect superparents. If Barry's dad can be a hotshot lawyer and pull in $200,000 a year, why can't my dad? If Karen's parents take her on neat vacations twice a year and sit around on weekends and listen to her problems, why can't mine? When parents don't come through, teens feel mistreated and depressed.

In addition to unreal expectations of self and parents, teens sometimes expect too much from their friends. Having so many expectations leads to disappointment. Friends are not *always* there when you need them. They go out of town for the weekend when you need to talk about boyfriend problems. They go to parties even when you aren't invited.

When you expect things of people and they don't come through for you, there's always implied criticism. When friends feel this criticism through a comment or hurt expression, they may withdraw even further due to guilt.

"But the funny thing is that as I see mental health, you could almost characterize it by the ability to tolerate inconsistency," writes Jess Lair in *I ain't much, baby—but I'm all I've got*. Friends will be inconsistent. They will ask for a ride with you and then at the last minute decide to go with someone else. They will stay by your side all night and then leave your party before time to clean up. They will talk you into trying out for varsity, and then complain that you don't have time for them now because you're always gone to ball games.

Wrapping all your emotions, goals, interests in a little box and handing it to friends for safekeeping is bound to lead to disappointment.

BOREDOM.

A chief cause of depression in our day, boredom results from too much time and too little purpose. When you're out worrying about picking up enough aluminum cans to pay for food, you don't have to worry about "meaningful" relationships. But when you have ten dollars allowance to spend as you please, then you have a problem choosing an album that you really want.

Depression caused by boredom sneaks up on you. You often hear people call it the blahs. They're describing an emptiness in their lives because they have no goal, nothing to accomplish that they consider worthy of their time.

People who have no goals and no interests are also boring to be around. If you feel bored, you're probably depressing others as well as yourself.

POOR HEALTH AND NO EXERCISE.

Just as a worried mind can make a sick body (migraines, obesity, alcoholism, ulcers, high blood pressure), sick bodies can make depressed minds. Proper diet, rest, and exercise go a long way in relieving depression. When you live on junk foods, you feel jittery, worried, and uptight about things that the body with proper nutrition could take in stride.

You cannot cut the link between the two—mind and body. A physically fit body goes a long way in dispelling depression.

HOW TO OVERCOME DEPRESSION

- I get depressed a lot at night. Sleep helps me escape. Sometimes I come in during the afternoon and just take a nap, too.
- When I'm depressed I gain ten pounds in one week. Then I really feel terrible about myself and am bombarded with horrible feelings.
- I usually get depressed when I'm home by myself so I watch a lot of TV or read.
- When I get home and most of my friends are still in school, I get depressed. When I get out early, I just go smoke a joint.

These solutions—TV, food, drugs, reading, sleep—mask the real causes of depression rather than clear them up.

But some teens, rather than trying to hide the depression from themselves, try other defenses. Eileen explains her brooding moods this way: "I'm not like other people. I'm the serious type and it just doesn't turn me on to go to a lot of parties. I like to get in touch with my lonely feelings. That's just the way I am."

Analyzing why you are as you are usually leads to justification and perpetuates the depression. And resigning yourself to depression could eventually lead to suicide.

To overcome depression, *you have to do something about it.*

Teens often don't realize this and describe their depression in terms of "something just came over me" or "I just started to feel bad but then after a while it passed." People who overcome depressed feelings with little trouble—whether they're conscious of their efforts for coping or not—*do* something to feel better.

Now, before you say that it won't work (as is characteristic of many chronically lonely and depressed people) read through the suggestions below and the testimonies of many teens who find that they *can* control their own feelings.

Some teens psyche themselves out of bad feelings:

- Sometimes I just say, "do you really have a reason? Look at all these things around you, and all your friends. You're lucky."
- I just always say, "what's the worst thing that can happen?" For example, I was depressed and worried about failing English. I mean it was killing me. I just said, "Okay, what's the worst? I fail the course and I have to go to summer school. So my dad has

to rearrange vacation. He'll holler, but he's done that before. What's summer school—five weeks? I can stand anything for five weeks." Once you get the worst out of the way, it's all over.

• I try to find something to look forward to and force myself to think about that.

But for many, sheer positive thinking doesn't drive away depression. They need something more, and that something more is action.

The following are suggestions from therapists and teens who have, through trial and error, found what actions work for them:

1. *Keep up with your normal routine and stay busy.* When you're upset, staying alone to brood is the worst thing you can do. Your mind dredges up unhappy memories and you become more miserable. Problems grow until they seem insurmountable.

• When I get down, I go out with my friends to a party or something and joke around and try to have fun.
• When I get depressed (about twice a week), I just get in the car and go shopping or something.
• I've just moved and have no close friends and I miss companionship. I overcome this by keeping busy, listening to records, reading, whatever.

You'd be surprised how much willpower you can muster to keep up with your routine and act your way into a new feeling. If you have no routine, develop one.

2. *Work or exercise.* Hard work is one of the best ways to overcome loneliness and isolation. If you don't have a paid job, look for odd jobs around the house. Does your mother's recipe file need reworking? Does the trim on the house need paint? Does your little brother need shelves in the closet to hold his games? Could you sort, label, and assemble family photos into albums? Could you collect your favorite poems and song lyrics into a notebook for your grandmother? There's work to do all around you.

In the absence of work, try strenuous exercise. Teens who said they exercised their way through depression mentioned shooting baskets, sparring, jogging, biking, and punching a bag.

I repeat, your mind and body are linked—heal one by using the other.

3. *Indulge yourself.* Occasionally, if you do not make this a habitual way of coping, you can alleviate depression by taking time to be kind to yourself, sharing your problems, or even wallowing in self-pity.

- When I get down, I call up my friends and tell them my problems and cry my eyeballs out. It helps, I always feel better when I hang up.
- I go out and buy and buy and buy new clothes.
- I do an overall beauty treatment—a shampoo, manicure, pedicure, try new makeup.

You perhaps have found other ways to pamper yourself—treating yourself to a movie, going out for a banana split, taking a long nap in the sun. As long as your indulgences don't complicate your problem by making you brood, adding to a weight problem, burdening your friends, or destroying your budget, they can carry you over *temporary* down-in-the-dumps feelings.

4. Work out a problem-solving technique. If depressed feelings keep haunting you, possibly you have not quite got your finger on the cause of the problem. It's easier to think that depression "just came over you," than to look for something you did or didn't do. But once you find the cause, you can work out a solution once and for all.

If you're constantly depressed over grades, break the problem down into parts. What subjects give you trouble? Is it daily work or exams? Can you talk to the counselor about a tutor? Can you rearrange your time at home and make more time for study?

If you're depressed over your looks—weight, hair, posture—work on some of the grooming tips given in Chapter 4 or find other information to correct or camouflage your problem.

If you don't get along with a particular person, can you arrange to get a schedule change or drop out of the activity that brings you into confrontation?

If your problem is boredom, talk to your counselor about extracurricular activities and service clubs that might interest you. One teen finds fulfillment working with the mentally retarded: "I used to get very depressed, but last year I started working with profoundly retarded adults and realized I have no right to ever be depressed. These people cope and are happy with what they have. Whenever I begin to feel depressed, I think of this and am thankful for what I have."

Find a cause to care about. Does your school need to begin fund-raising for new trophy cases? Is there an elderly person in your neighborhood who would appreciate a daily visit? Can you talk to your counselor about setting up a hotline for troubled teens, staffed by high school volunteers who've gone through counseling training? Can you condition yourself to run a marathon by next spring? Can you volunteer to be a big brother or sister to an underprivileged child? Could your church youth group leader use a volunteer to make phone calls or draw posters?

5. *Talk to a counselor.* How do you know if you need to talk over your problems with a trained school counselor, a minister, or a therapist? The following list of questions may help:

1. Have you lost interest in things you used to enjoy?
2. Do you have trouble concentrating in school or on work you are supposed to do?
3. Do you have trouble sleeping at night?
4. Do you cry a lot?
5. Have you lost your appetite?

6. Are you constantly angry and irritable?
7. Do you have thoughts of harming your-self?

Often people are hesitant to go to a counselor because they're ashamed that they have problems and want to feel as "normal" as everybody else.

But who knows what normal is? Everybody could profit from talking with a counselor now and then to gain a new perspective on life. Therapists often say they have many "normal" people who come to see them only to work out small problems and expand their understanding about themselves. We all need help and advice from friends and family at times, but someone with special training may be necessary for your particular situation.

Don't let money stand in your way. Call your mental health association listed in the phone book and they will arrange for you to pay whatever you can afford.

Anger, guilt, unreal expectations, boredom, lack of exercise—all the causes of depression should actually make you hopeful because you can control your feelings by controlling these causes and your reactions to them.

Aloneness gives you opportunity to polish your personality. But feeling lonely indicates the need to change or incorporate something new in your life.

WHAT THEN IS HAPPY?

The absence of depression doesn't necessarily mean happiness. Author of the bestseller

Pathfinders, Gail Sheehy surveyed 60,000 people nationwide to put together a profile of the contented person. Here is what those she talked with had to say about feeling satisfied with life:

1. My life has meaning and direction.
2. I have experienced one or more important transitions in my life (death, moving, divorce, etc.) and I have handled these in a personal, creative way.
3. I rarely feel cheated or disappointed by life.
4. I have already attained several long-term goals important to me.
5. I am pleased with my personal growth and development.
6. I am in love, and my partner and I love each other mutually.
7. I have many friends.
8. I am a cheerful person.
9. I am not thin-skinned or sensitive to criticism.
10. I have no major fears.

Notice that the number one distinguishing factor in these people's lives was direction. To some that means religious faith; to others, a humanitarian cause; to others, work projects; to others, helping family or friends.

In my own survey of high schoolers, teens underscored the same idea, saying their faith in God or accomplishing something important made them feel content. One seventeen-year old girl summed it up this way: "I make myself happy. I feel like no one can cheer you up except yourself.

If you don't want to be happy, you won't be happy. It's all in your attitude."

Take charge of your life rather than letting circumstances or other people dictate your emotions. When you lose yourself in a cause larger than yourself, happiness will "happen" to you when you least expect it.

Chapter Nine

INTO EVERY LIFE
SOME REJECTION
MUST FALL

EVERYONE FACES REJECTION at some time in his life. Job applicants get turned down, presidents are voted out of office, actors star in box-office flops, and athletes get booed off the field. Often this rejection has little to do with the individual rejected, but rather involves the circumstances or the rejector.

Some people reject others thinking that by tearing others down they can build themselves up. Others reject because they are thoughtless, prejudiced, or ignorant.

Whatever the reason, rejection hurts:

> • I'm often ridiculed, teased, cut down by my peers. It's common. I'm very sensitive and I, in turn, make them feel not so hot. If this doesn't work, I just have to go along with it.
> • Yes, ridicule makes me angry—like I want to beat them up.
> • They reject me because I'm not really

177

popular, and I feel inadequate because of
no money, and looks mostly. I hate it! I try
to make it go away. But it doesn't.

Rejection comes from different directions. For
some teens, it's parents who make them feel inadequate:

- Me and my father aren't close and at times I
  feel really rejected because he doesn't do
  things with me—always my little brother.
  And my mother never pays any attention to
  me—only to my little brother. But my
  brother and I are close most of the time. I
  tell my parents that I need love, too.
- My parents reject my attitude and my feelings about life. I go and cry and then talk to
  myself and tell myself I'm good enough for
  me.
- I don't make good grades, and I'm not
  going to college. I just tell myself that when
  I get out of school, they [parents] won't bug
  me anymore.
- My parents reject everything about me.
  They can't stand me. That's why I ran away
  from home.

For teens who have to deal with such intense
parental rejection, perhaps it will help to remember that parents have an imperfect love or no
love at all because of something within themselves, not necessarily because of something
within the teen. Some parents reject traits within
you because they hate the same traits in themselves. Some parents try to relive their life
through you by pressuring you to be something

they were not—an athletic star, a brain, or a beauty. They feel like failures themselves if you don't make the spotlight.

Teachers can also make you feel rejected with cutting or sarcastic comments on a paper, by the way they talk or don't talk to you, or by the way they look or don't look at you:

> • I had this Spanish homework assignment to translate some sentences. And I was having a hard time doing them. In some of the sentences, I just left out chunks of words and wrote down which words I knew and what they meant. Well, when I got the paper back, the teacher had written sarcastic remarks like, "You call this English?" I was so embarrassed. She did that all semester. I hated that teacher after that.
>
> • I feel that some of my teachers reject me because I'm richer or have nicer things and drive a nicer car, etc., than they do.
>
> • Teachers get mad at me because I'm a jock and they think that *I think* I can get away with anything.

Contrary to popular belief, teachers are human and they react much like the rest of the world. If you cause trouble in the classroom, they may want to get revenge. If you don't do well on an exam, they may make you feel stupid because they don't want to face the fact that maybe they didn't teach the subject well. If they perceive through your body language (you sit at the back of the room, refuse to talk in class, don't look them in the eye) that you reject them, they, in turn, may give you the silent treatment. And teachers may reject you for other personal reasons—they have the same faults they see in you or you remind them of someone else they dislike. You may get a cold shoulder for any number of reasons.

But for most teens, the most damaging rejection comes from peers. When I asked teens in the survey to tell me about rejection they felt from parents and teachers, many responded, "Who cares?" But an uncaring defense was much less common when these same teens mentioned rejection by others in their own age group. Teenage is a time for finding out who you are, and that identity often comes from filtering out peers' opinions of you.

Chris remembers a putdown: "When I was in ninth grade, I wore this green shirt, and everybody started making fun of it and me. I felt really stupid. I tried to hide the rest of the day, and I never wore it again."

If rejection can make you feel so devastated, then it's important to understand why and how to cope without letting it destroy your self-confidence. Teens have shared the following reasons for rejection. Perhaps you can gain some insight into why people may reject you for similar reasons:

MORAL DIFFERENCES

- I don't get invited many places and my mom is always on my back about it. And so I told her why—that the rest of the kids

smoke pot, and drink, and sleep around.
Boy, she shut up fast.

• I shouldn't feel rejected I guess, but when
all my friends are going out, I never go
since I don't drink. So now they never even
ask me. I wouldn't go, so I can understand
them in a way. But even to parties, they
don't bother to ask me anymore.

Many teens find themselves in similar isolation
for moral reasons. If you don't drink, smoke pot,
or sleep around, your presence may make those
who do feel condemned because they inwardly
don't like what they are doing. Particularly, they
may pressure you if they themselves were pressured into the activity and don't feel right about it.

Often teens feel that those who don't participate in their lifestyle look down on them and believe themselves to be better. Still others don't
want to be around you because they think you
don't know how to have a good time—at least by
their standards.

RELIGIOUS DIFFERENCES

One teen explains: "Because I'm a Christian now,
I take a stand for that. Some people say that I'm a
Christian 'freak,' and I feel hurt. But I also know I
can't compromise what I feel is right."

Jews, Mormons, and many other religious
groups have experienced their share of rejection.
People tend to view anyone different from them
as "way out" or "freakish." Sometimes, when you

celebrate different days of worship and different holidays from the majority, you get left out of school or community activities. To some, different is bad.

Other teens have no faith in their life at all and see religion as a foolish endeavor and a crutch that "strong" people don't need. Others reject religious people because they feel condemned about their own lack of belief and convictions. Making others feel foolish is a way of making themselves feel wise.

DISABILITIES

"I can understand being rejected because of my handicap," explains one teen involved in a motorcycle accident and paralyzed from the waist down, "but sometimes I just can't accept it."

Another teen says, "When I was younger, I had severely crossed eyes, but I had perfect vision. My peers called me 'retarded.' I knew this wasn't true, so I tried to ignore them. I felt bad and stupid and generally inferior."

A large part of the population has some sort of disability—from bad eyesight, to hearing loss, to a crippled limb, to a stutter. But some teens decide that some flaws are "normal" and others are tragic. Most people do not willfully reject those who have a disability, but they shy away from them because of an unconscious fear that the same "tragedy" might happen to them.

Selfishness is a second reason teens may shy

away from you if you are disabled. If they
have to push your wheelchair, they can't be first
in line at the ticket counter. Finally, they may be
lacking in self-confidence themselves and fear
that associating with anyone different in any way
may hurt their own chances for acceptance.

Usually, acceptance into a group is based on
conformity, companionship, and recognition for
skills. If someone can't compete in these ways, he
or she is often left out.

RACE

Stereotypes abound because people don't take
time to get to know those of another race personally. All blacks aren't lazy, all whites aren't bigots,
all Japanese aren't hard workers, all Jews aren't
rich—any more than *all* teens are pot smokers,
rude, or energetic.

Why do people feel prejudiced against other
races? Some learn prejudice from parents and
teachers. Others have never been around people
of another race, and unfamiliarity leads to irra-
tional fears.

LEVELS OF MATURITY

"Boys used to tease me when I was in junior high
because I didn't have a figure. I was always so
skinny, and I really hurt until I got into high
school. Now, as a junior, I don't have a problem,"
says Marilyn.

Girls get teased if they have no figure and if they have too much of a figure—either way they lose. Boys, too, get their share of teasing, being called runt, pipsqueak and the like. Being physically different can even eliminate you from such activities as sports. More teens push the panic button about their growth rate than any other trait, skill, or condition. And because of the hopelessly insecure feeling some teens have about their size, they point a finger at everyone else, hoping to direct attention away from themselves. If they can point out someone else who is fatter or thinner, taller or shorter than they are, then they become "average" and safe.

MONEY AND STATUS

Poverty is always relative. You're poor if everybody but you has two pairs of shoes, and you're poor if everyone but you has a tennis court in the backyard.

No doubt about it, money opens doors even as early as kindergarten. You don't get chosen for the school play if your parents can't afford the butterfly suit. In junior high you don't try out for cheerleader if you can't afford cheerleading camp. In senior high you don't date if you can't afford transportation and/or the price of two movie tickets.

Some people place much importance on money

or social status because they're taught at home that possessions make superior people. Others reject those who have less because they feel inadequate in some other area, and they flaunt their money to build their own self-esteem. Some operate under the illusion that money means intelligence or skill. They have never considered that others may have less money because they have different values—they spend more time with family than on the job or give more to church or charity than they spend on house and clothes.

Some, although often late in life, finally learn that money isn't spoken everywhere.

APPEARANCE

- I had gotten a pair of large, plastic designer frame glasses in the seventh grade. Some of the guys made fun of them. I felt very embarrassed and bad about myself. I felt like I wasn't as good as others.
- I get rejected because of my overweight problem. People look at my body and not at my mind and personality. I'm a really fun person, but a lot of people don't know that.
- They call me moon-man, crater-face. I feel really bad.
- When I was in eighth grade, all the kids on the bus made fun of me because I had blond curly hair. They used to call me names and throw paper at me. I remember thinking I must be ugly for them to say

those things and I had a complex about my hair for a long time after that.

I think it would be hard to find even ten percent of the population who have not been teased about their appearance—from floppy ears, to a little mouth. Teens reject others' appearance when they feel insecure about their own.

This hostility raging within someone who is unable to correct his or her "defect" spills over to anybody else who seems vulnerable to attack. This person keeps yelling that somebody else's boat is on fire, hoping that nobody will ignite his own.

PARENTAL EMBARRASSMENTS

The daughter of a pro ball player: "I get put down about my dad. He's my idol and when something bad is said, I go into defense. After a loss in a football game, school is always terrible. Kids are so cruel and make fun of how he plays." This problem shows that not only do people put down the down-and-out, but often, out of jealousy, they pick on those who are in a prestigious spot.

Of course, having an alcoholic or criminal parent whom others read about in the newspaper can also bring rejection. Some teens stay away from an alcoholic's son or daughter because they feel that bad habits or attitudes may rub off on them. And, of course, fear of a bad reputation keeps others away. Although these same people would balk at being judged by their own parents' accomplishments, skills, and personalities, they never think of affording you the same courtesy of judging you on your own merits.

Before deciding to live with rejection for any of these reasons, make very sure that it's not your *attitude* about your "difference" that makes people reject you rather than the "difference" itself. Below is a checklist that may give you some insight about how and why others may react with indifference and contempt:

REJECTION ATTITUDE CHECKLIST

Morals

1. Do you frequently point out rather than downplay your lack of participation— smoking, drinking, cussing, cheating?
2. Do you leave the impression that you're better than people who have what you consider "low" morals?
3. Do you try to force your values on others when they don't want your opinion of what they're doing?

Religion

4. Do you argue that your religious beliefs are correct and that everyone else's beliefs are wrong?
5. Do you present a "holier-than-thou" attitude?

Disabilities

6. Do you pity yourself about what you can't do and complain to those around

you?

7. Do you use your disability to get sympathy and special privileges?
8. Do you *demand* help and attention rather than *ask* for it?

Race

9. Do you tend to stand, sit, and eat alone as though you were suspicious of those of another race?
10. Do you project the idea that you'd rather be with "your own"?
11. Do you make any effort to counter undesirable stereotypes?

Maturity

12. Do you "pester" people with childish pranks which highlight your small size?
13. Do you try to make those less mature jealous because you look older?

Money and Status

14. Do you announce your lack of spending money and your envy?
15. Do you make others feel guilty about having more?

Appearance

16. Do you flaunt less-than-perfect features by poor grooming habits—like wearing tight clothes that call attention to bulges?
17. Do you give the impression that you don't care about your appearance by poor diet and exercise habits?
18. Do you purposely dress out of style to project the image that you don't care

about fashion and that those who do are
frivolous and vain?

Parental Embarrassments

19. Do you isolate yourself by being secretive and by never inviting friends over
because your mother might be drunk
when they arrive?
20. Do you become defensive when others
comment on your parent or the bad
habit?

Most people respect high morals—as long as
they don't feel condemned themselves. And religion in itself is rarely cause for rejection; consider
the respect shown to present-day clergymen and
religious leaders.

Most disabled people make others uncomfortable about the disability only when they feel uncomfortable about it themselves. Self-acceptance
refurbishes the outer flaw.

Race is a common divider, but time and educa-
tion will help.

As with racial rejection, time corrects maturity
problems.

Although many people feel awkward about
someone else's financial misfortunes, you can put
the people at ease by showing that you are not
jealous and by being enthusiastic about good fortune and opportunities.

And, everybody has facial and figure defects—
it's how you camouflage them or accept them that
affects the way people see you.

Finally, ask yourself whether you pick your

friends according to what you think of their parents? Probably not. Neither do most teens. If necessary, remind others that you are not your parent who has the bad habit. If you want to bring a friend home with you, you can always say something like: "My mother drinks a lot, and I don't know how she will be when we get inside." That lets the friend know that you are your own person and that you do not consider yourself responsible for her condition.

Your attitude about your "difference" can dictate isolation and rejection by those around you. The wrong tone of voice, facial expression, or posture can bring out hostilities in others that would never surface otherwise.

A small minority of teens actually like to suffer rejection. For one thing, the reaction is familiar—they don't have to learn to be socially acceptable and to please others. And keeping things the same can be comfortable, even if sad. But probably the biggest payoff in suffering is that the "difference" provides an excuse for things that could, with effort, be corrected.

The majority, however, who experience rejection would like to overcome it—at least to handle it in a nondestructive way.

How?

1. *Like yourself.* This one trait—a poor self-image—makes you more vulnerable to rejection than anything else.

"I felt low, low down on myself," says Gary. "Like I wasn't as good as anybody else there.

Like I couldn't even improve. I feel unwanted and low class."

Nobody can make you feel inferior without your permission. Learn to psyche yourself up and feel comfortable about your differences as these high schoolers have done:

- I'm not a partier or drinker. . . .Some people wish they could say no to drinking, too.
- I have always had big feet for my age. They would cut me down because of this, but I didn't let it bother me. To me, people tease others because they aren't confident of themselves.
- I get rejected because of my appearance and no money. But it's not the outside of you that counts. It's the inside.
- Sometimes people tease me because I'm so skinny, but I don't consider that ridicule really. I consider it envy because they'd like to be thinner.
- I don't go out and party with kids because that is just not me. Most of the time I hang around with kids from church. I feel like I am benefiting from staying out of the drugs and alcohol scene. I'll be a better person in the end.

Whatever you feel—that the issue is unimportant, that you're happy anyway, that you have courage to say no, that others actually envy you—doesn't matter. As long as you feel good about yourself, you will survive.

2. *When people tease you, try to have a*

sense of humor and don't let them know the teasing bothers you. Listen to the *way* they tease rather than what they say. Generally, people tease only people they like, and they may not know you are particularly sensitive in one particular area.

If something looks funny, admit it looks funny. Don't always interpret humorous remarks as derogatory, as if the person willfully is out to hurt you. People laugh at funny "failures" sometimes just as they laugh at slapstick accidents on TV.

Another way to defuse teasing is to admit your failure or weakness. When you seem down, most people reach out in sympathy to lift you up. When you fight to stay on top, they often get the impulse to hold your head underwater.

Finally, if the teasing turns malicious, you may have to confront the teaser. If someone tells you that you're the lousiest skater he's ever seen, tell him that you've registered his complaint or that he's welcome to his own dumb opinion. If you feel like it, you can tell him your own views.

It's your reaction to teasing that determines the end result.

3. *When you feel rejected, try to remove yourself from the painful situation.* Life is too short to suffer persecution needlessly. Some might say that a more courageous person would stay in the situation and fight to the bitter end. However, life shouldn't be competition but coexistence. If other band members make fun of your playing and band practice becomes a drudgery, get out. If the group leader always

makes you the butt of the jokes or the go-fer, find another group to hang around with.

4. *Find supportive friends who have similar interests, backgrounds, morals, or problems.* People who share the same religious faith will understand your desire to adhere to religious tenets. Those who live in leg braces can understand and talk to you about problems in getting in the mainstream of school activities. People who think like you can eliminate the pressure you feel to conform to those whose values or behavior you don't want to imitate.

5. *Try to win over your opposition.* Be genuine in your conversation and behavior. Many people think that someone who acts differently is phony. Make sure they know you are not trying to put on a freak act for attention.

Try to show interest in and encourage your enemy. In other words, step out of the spotlight and put him inside the lighted circle. A person who otherwise might insult you will generally relinquish the floor to you if you want to talk about his accomplishments.

Do a favor for an enemy. Diane and Brenda had a long-standing rivalry going because Brenda was now dating Diane's former boyfriend. It was not that Diane was jealous, but rather that Brenda assumed she was and assumed that she wanted her old boyfriend back. Some months into the school year, Diane was elected Sweetheart of the Future Farmers of America Chapter and found out she would be making a weekend trip to a state convention with the club's officers (the ex-boyfriend was president). Although thrilled about the election and the trip, she dreaded the deep freeze from Brenda and her group. Allowed to invite one female friend to accompany her on the trip, Diane decided to ask Brenda to go along. She made her point—Brenda turned into an ally.

On the other hand, you might try asking a favor of your opposition. Ask for an after-school ride home or ask for help with your math homework. To make such a request, you have to swallow your pride and that appeals to the other person's vanity. Often a favor request will break the ice quicker than generosity on your part.

In summary, avoid vulnerability to rejection by feeling good about yourself. Self-love is paramount in developing healthy relations with others. When teased, pay attention to the *way* you're teased rather than the words. Try to laugh at yourself and admit your own weaknesses. Remove yourself from unpleasant situations when necessary. Instead, surround yourself with supportive friends of similar persuasion. Finally, win over your opposition, if possible, by showing genuine interest rather than animosity.

CAN I REALLY BE A WINNER?

All the past should do is tell you what doesn't work. The future is yours for the living. One day at a time you can build a new self-image and a new reputation. Don't let those who look skeptical at your turning over a new leaf discourage you. Quietly, confidently, show them.

Bitterness only poisons you and those around you. Carolyn, 16, tells about her experience with a classmate: "At first, I try to include people who are left out, but there is this one girl in my home economics class. I try to be nice, but she is sometimes so bitter. She's like a big baby always wanting her way and if she doesn't get it, she pouts. However, she never gives encouragement to others and doesn't offer suggestions to group projects or anything. I try to tolerate her and usually end up ignoring her. I guess this is because she is an outcast and she brings it all on herself. She doesn't try to strive or smile or have patience. It's hard for me to return these things to her if she is so bitter."

Rather than withdrawing into yourself and wallowing in defeat, square your shoulders and learn from what's happened or what's happening around you. Many of society's adult successes were adolescent "failures" by their own and others' standards.

To live is to fail and be rejected. But prime-time living means growing into a better person day by day.

Bibliography

Ackerman, Paul, Ph. D., and Kappelman, Murray, M.D. *Signals. What Your Child Is Really Telling You*. New York: The Dial Press, 1978.

Anderson, J. D. *How to Stop Worrying About Your Kids*. New York: Norton, 1978.

Axum, Donna. *The Outer You*. Waco, Texas: Word, 1978.

Bailard, Virginia, and Strang, Ruth. *Ways to Improve Your Personality*. New York: McGraw-Hill, 1965.

Bellak, Leopold, M.D., and Baker, Samm Sinclair. *Reading Faces*. New York: Holt, Rinehart and Winston, 1981.

Berne, Eric, M.D. *What Do You Say After You Say Hello?* New York: Bantam, 1973.

Branden, Nathaniel. *The Disowned Self*. New York: Bantam, 1971.

Bry, Adelaide. *Friendship: How to Have a Friend and*

Be a Friend. New York: Grosset & Dunlap, 1979.

Carnegie, Dale. *How to Win Friends and Influence People.* New York: Pocket Books, 1936.

Clark, Kenneth B. *Prejudice and Your Child.* Boston: Beacon Press, 1955.

Coleman, Emily. *Making Friends with the Opposite Sex.* Los Angeles: Nash Publishing, 1972.

Conde, Bertha. *The Business of Being a Friend.* Boston and New York: Houghton Mifflin, 1916.

Coombs, H. Samm. *Teenage Survival Manual, How to Enjoy the Trip to Twenty.* Santa Monica, California: Discovery, 1977.

DeRosis, Helen A., M.D., and Pellegrino, Victoria Y. *The Book of Hope. How Women Can Overcome Depression.* New York: Bantam, 1976.

Emerson, Ralph Waldo. *Friendship.* New York: Revell.

Faber, Adele, and Mazlish, Elaine. *How to Talk So Kids Will Listen and Listen So Kids Will Talk.* New York: Rawson, Wade, 1980.

Fast, Julius. *Body Language.* New York: Pocket Books, 1970.

————. *The Body Language of Sex, Power and Aggression.* New York: M. Evans, 1977.

Fast, Julius, and Fast, Barbara. *Talking Between the Lines.* New York: Viking, 1979.

Fitzgerald, Ernest A. *How to Be a Successful Failure.* New York: Atheneum, 1978.

Gordon, Sol. *Living Fully: A Guide for Young People with a Handicap, Their Parents, Their Teachers, and Professionals.* New York: The John Day Co., 1975.

Gould, Shirley. *Teenagers: The Continuing Challenge.* New York: Hawthorn Books, 1977.

Greenwald, Jerry A., Ph.D. *Breaking Out of Loneliness*. New York: Rawson, Wade, 1980.

Grossman, Richard. *Choosing and Changing: A Guide to Self-Reliance*. New York: E. P. Dutton, 1978.

Hales, Celia, Ph.D., and Matteson, Roberta, Ph.D. *I've Done So Well—Why Do I Feel So Bad?* New York: Macmillan, 1978.

Hall, Edward T. *The Hidden Dimension*. Garden City, New York: Doubleday, 1966.

Hearn, Janice W. *Making Friends, Keeping Friends. How to Build Bridges Instead of Walls*. New York: Doubleday, 1979.

Igor, S. Kon, and Losenkov, Vladimir A. "Friendship in Adolescence: Values and Behavior." *Journal of Family and Marriage*. 40 (F, 1978), 143–55.

Kalb, Johan, and Viscott, David, M.D. *What Every Kid Should Know*. Boston: Houghton Mifflin, 1976.

Kandel, Denise B. "Similarity in Real-Life Adolescent Friendship Pairs." *Journal of Personality and Social Psychology*. 36 (March, 1978), 306–12.

Kiev, Ari, M.D. *Riding Through the Downers, Hassles, Snags, and Funks*. New York: E. P. Dutton, 1981.

Killinger, John R. *The Loneliness of Children*. New York: Vanguard, 1980.

Lair, Jess, Ph. D. *I ain't much, baby—but I'm all I've got*. Connecticut: Fawcett, 1969.

Lepp, Ignace. Tr. by Bernard Murchland. *The Ways of Friendship*. New York: Macmillan, 1966.

Lever, Janet. "Sex Differences in the Games Children Play." *Social Problems*. 23 (1976), 478–87.

Madison, Arnold. *Suicide*. New York: Clarion, 1978.

McGinnis, Alan Loy. "Excerpt from *The Friendship Factor*." *Good Housekeeping*. 189 (July, 1979), 110+.

Menninger, William C., M.D. et al. *How to Be a Successful Teen-ager*. New York: Sterling Publishing, 1966.

Mitchell, Joyce Slayton. *See Me More Clearly*. New York: Harcourt, Brace, Jovanovich, 1980.

Narramore, Bruce, Ph.D. *Adolescene Is Not an Illness*. New York: Revell, 1980.

Newman, Mildred, and Berkowitz, Bernard, with Jean Owen. *How to Be Your Own Best Friend*. New York: Ballantine, 1971.

Norman, Jane, and Harris, Myron, Ph.D. *The Private Life of the American Teenager*. New York: Rawson, Wade, 1981.

Parlee, Mary Brown. "The Friendship Bond." *Psychiatric Opinion*. 13 (October, 1979) 43–54+.

Purkey, William W. *Self-Concept and School Achievement*. Englewood Cliffs, New Jersey: Prentice-Hall, 1970.

Richards, Arlene Kramer, and Willis, Irene. *Boy Friends, Girl Friends, Just Friends*. New York: Atheneum, 1979.

Rosenberg, Morris. *Conceiving the Self*. New York: Basic Books, 1979.

Rubin, Zick. *Children's Friendships*. Massachusetts: Harvard University Press, 1980.

Schultz, Terri. *Bittersweet: Surviving and Growing from Loneliness*. New York: Thomas Y. Crowell, 1976.

Segerstrom, Jane. *Look Like Yourself and Love It*. Houston: Triad Press, 1980.

Sheehy, Gail. *Pathfinders.* New York: Morrow, 1981.

Shelmire, Bedford, Jr. *The Art of Being Beautiful at Any Age.* New York: St. Martin's Press, 1975.

Siegel, Ernest, Rita, and Paul. *Help for the Lonely Child: Strengthening Social Perception.* New York: Sunrise, 1978.

Skoglund, Elizabeth. *Beyond Loneliness.* New York: Doubleday, 1980.

Stern, Barbara Lang. "How to Set—and Reach—Goals for Yourself." *Vogue.* 171 (July, 1981), 80–81.

Terrone, Maria. "Can Close Friends Ever Be Too Close?" *Seventeen.* 79 (October, 1979), 142–43.

Wagenvoord, James, ed. *The Man's Book: A Complete Manual of Style.* New York: Avon, 1978.

Walters, Barbara. *How to Talk with Practically Anybody About Practically Anything.* New York: Doubleday, 1970.

Wood, Abigail. *The Seventeen Book of Answers to What Your Parents Don't Talk About and Your Best Friends Can't Tell You.* New York: David McKay, 1972.

Zimbardo, Philip G. *Shyness: What It Is. What To Do About It.* Reading, Massachusetts: Addison-Wesley Publishing, 1977.

INDEX

Index

Index

ABOUT THE AUTHOR

DIANNA DANIELS BOOHER holds a BA degree from North Texas State University and a MA degree from the University of Houston, both degrees in English literature. She has worked extensively with young people, both as a teacher in public schools and together with her husband, who is a church youth director.

Ms. Booher has published curriculum materials as well as numerous magazine articles. She has also published four self-help books, *Coping ... When Your Family Falls Apart, Help, We're Moving, The Faces of Death*, and *Rape: What Would You Do If ... ?*; two novels, *Not Yet Free* and *The Last Caress;* and a business book, *Would You Put That in Writing: How to Write Your Way to Business Success*. Ms. Booher also conducts business writing workshops with her own firm, Booher Writing Consultants. Reviewing books for the *Houston Chronicle* rounds out her writing activities.

Ms. Booher lives in Houston, Texas, with her husband, Dan, and two children, Jeffrey and Lisa.